THE MAN FROM PLAINS

THE MAN FROM PLAINS

A Portrait of Jimmy Carter

David Kucharsky

COLLINS
St James's Place, London
1977

William Collins Sons & Co Ltd
London · Glasgow · Sydney · Auckland
Toronto · Johannesburg

Grateful acknowledgement is extended to *Christianity Today* for permission to use as a portion of chapter 4 material from the article 'Careers With Christian Impact', which appeared in the issue of 24th September 1971; to Broadman Press for permission to quote from *Why Not The Best?* by Jimmy Carter, copyright © 1975 by Broadman Press; and to the *Alliance Witness* for permission to incorporate an article that I prepared initially for its Bicentennial issue.

First published in Great Britain 1977
First published 1976

ISBN 0 00 216507 4

Made and Printed in Great Britain by
William Collins Sons & Co Ltd Glasgow

Contents

Preface
1. The Outspoken Man of Conviction . . . 1
2. From Plains, Georgia . . . 25
3. Who Believes . . . 45
4. That It Is Time . . . 71
5. For Outsiders . . . 92
6. To Act Intelligently . . . 115
7. And Bring America Back Where She Belongs. 134
Epilogue 145

To Brenda
whose interest
kindled my own

Preface

This book attempts to unravel the mysteries of Jimmy Carter's extraordinary success story as well as to provide guidelines for understanding and evaluating the man and his thinking. The thirty-ninth President of the United States draws upon modern insights extensively, but not at the expense of time-honored truths. Why and how such a mix captivated so many so quickly is what the following pages are about.

The year of 1976 seemed to be the year of the evangelical. The reader will find in *The Man from Plains* an exploration not only of Carter but of the American mood which buoyed his ascent. Jimmy Carter cannot be adequately explained unless one gains some familiarity with the evangelical ethos, with its special focus upon being born again, which has never been far from the heart of the American experience. This presentation is designed so that Protestants, Catholics, Orthodox, and Jews—as well as unbelievers—can readily relate to these concepts.

Also helpful to a grasp of Carter is some fresh perspective on the age-old tension between church and state, which in modern America translates into the hesitation to mix religion and politics. Good fences may make good neighbors, but in politics, the suppression of religious opinions, or the distortion of them by untrained observers, can have serious consequences. The public needs to know their leaders' deepest motivations—the dangers that may lurk therein or the positive potential they may offer.

The value of this book will be enhanced if the reader thinks of it as a sorting out process. It does not take an exhaustive approach to biography and simply feed one fact about Carter's life after another. That approach has some merit, because there is a lot about Carter that has not yet been made public. My own tack, however, is the essay form because it seems to me to be what the novelty and complexity of the situation calls for. I try to provide perspective and to evaluate what is most significant without resorting to the extremes of hatchet jobs on the one hand or flatulent puffery on the other. A maze of raw data, after all, is in itself quite useless. We cannot form accurate and meaningful impressions if we do not see how things fit together. Francis Bacon said that "Truth will sooner come out from error than from confusion."

I have tried to level with the reader, and to leave as little as possible to the imagination. There is nothing coming up on the blind side, no sinister message hidden under a cloak of objectivity. Such subtleties may have their place, but not here. The issues surrounding Jimmy Carter are too serious and the consequences too far reaching to risk beating around a rhetorical bush.

For assorted help, I am especially grateful to my very patient and loving wife, to my children, to present and past colleagues at *Christianity Today,* to the cooperative people of Harper & Row, to all the good folks at Arlington Memorial Church, and to other friends. I certainly cannot claim to speak for any of them, but in the interest of candor it must be said that for good or ill they have helped shape my opinions! The Carter staff provided some assistance also, which I hereby acknowledge with appreciation. I am also prayerfully thankful for the country of which I am a part and honored to have been able to take on a project related to its destiny on the occasion of its two-hundredth birthday.

David Kucharsky

INTRODUCTION

As I discovered on a recent visit to America, everyone seems to be talking about President Carter. This is especially the case on campuses and at Washington tea parties. What is more, instead of the talk following the usual course when a new man enters the White House, and concerning itself with appointments, relations with Congress, that sort of thing, this time it is largely about the new President's evangelical Christianity and how being born again may be expected to influence him as Chief Executive. When John F. Kennedy was campaigning for the presidency he went out of his way to give assurances that his being a practising Roman Catholic would in no way affect the policies he would follow if elected. In President Carter's case, on the other hand, it is taken for granted that the Bible rather than the works of Keynes or Professor Galbraith will be the book he turns to for guidance in undertaking his new responsibilities. I confess it gave me a feeling of quiet satisfaction to imagine the media pundits, after their Watergate jamboree, feeling bound to struggle with Isaiah and Jeremiah, not to mention the Gospels and the Book of Revelation, and to bone up on predestination and justification by works, in forming their assessment of President Carter and his way of looking at things.

It is thus highly appropriate that one of the first books endeavouring to explain the Carter phenomenon should come, not from a Theodore H. White who has celebrated the three previous presidential elections with his *The Making of the President* volumes, nor even from some old White House hand like Arthur Schlesinger, but from the editor of an evangelical magazine *(Christianity Today),* David Kucharsky.

What he sets out to do in *The Man From Plains* is, putting aside all the Menckenesque ridiculing of the Bible Belt, and memories of William Jennings Bryan and the Scopes Trial as portrayed by the media, to explain just what an American Evangelical like President Carter may be assumed to believe, and how he relates his politics and political career to a strongly held Christian faith running counter to current trends in that, scripturally, it is fundamentalist, and in relation to contemporary *mores,* puritanical. As Kucharsky points out, this was the position the President took during his electoral campaign, and that he has continued to take since he came to the White House, with the result that views which until quite recently provided a ready supply of talk-show jokes have suddenly become a live issue on Capitol Hill. For the first time in the history of the United States the authentic voice of evangelical Christianity is heard, not just at Moody and Sankey revivalist conventions and Billy Graham crusades, but in the very citadel of American power, Washington DC.

It is difficult to think of an historical parallel for so curious a development, but re-reading recently Gibbon's famous chapter on the conversion to Christianity of the Emperor Constantine and the subsequent legal establishment and constitution of the Catholic Church, it occurred to me that there was a certain similarity between a pagan emperor becoming a Christian and a born-again Christian like Jimmy Carter becoming an emperor – which is what becoming President of the United States amounts to. The two events, in any case, have given rise to the same sort of controversy. Did the Emperor Constantine become a Christian sympathizer and ultimately a baptized Christian himself for policy reasons or because of a genuine acceptance of Christ as his saviour? Gibbon examines the question with his usual wit and elegance, and inevitably comes down on the policy side. Many Americans are likewise asking themselves whether President Carter exploited his conversion and Southern Baptist affiliations to help his presidential candidature. Or was it that he just felt impelled to make his born-again record part of his electoral strategy whatever the electoral consequences, and that in the post-Watergate situation it worked.

The question remains open, and David Kucharsky is much too sensible to attempt at this stage a definitive answer as to whether President Carter's Christian faith is an adjunct to his political purposes or vice versa. What he does do is to help readers to sort the prospects out, showing that the President is neither a religious brontosaurus who belongs to a vanished past, nor a political adventurer who sees in evangelical Christianity, with its large and ardent following, especially among the coloured population, a useful acquisition of strength. Rather, he sees him as a perfectly sincere Christian, ready to admit to his own failings and inadequacies, aware that the realm of politics belongs to the children of darkness and requires compromises which are spiritually and often ethically inadmissible, and that deciding what is due to Caesar and what to God is particularly difficult when you happen to be Caesar yourself.

I asked a seasoned observer of the Washington scene who was not particularly well disposed towards the Carter regime whether he agreed with me tnat up to now the President has not done anything which was politically maladroit or religiously hypocritical. He grudgingly agreed. David Kucharsky obviously goes much further than this, and sees in President Carter's election the beginning of a true recovery of spiritual values, a turning away from the sordid materialism and hedonism which has characterized the American way of life in recent years. I hope with all my heart he may be right, and recommend his book as a clear and honest presentation of the new Carter setup in Washington whose coming is of enormous importance for the rest of the world, and especially for the countries of Western Europe.

Malcolm Muggeridge
June 1977

1

The Outspoken Man of Conviction . . .

ON A clear, hot Sunday morning in June, Jimmy Carter and twelve other members of the men's Sunday school class of Plains Baptist Church met for their regular weekly session. Thirteen visitors, most of them curious newsmen, also were on hand. They crowded out the little room on the second story of the church. Carter and the class officers sat around the table at one end. Sunshine poured through the venetian blinds, and a single 200-watt light bulb glowed from the white ceiling. The off-white room with a dark brown floor was austere and impeccably clean. As Kandy Stroud said in the *Washington Star* of a similar class which Carter had addressed a few months before, "It seemed a strangely New Testament setting for a presidential candidate."

It was a week before the nation's two-hundredth birthday and barely two weeks before the Democratic National Convention was scheduled to nominate Carter for president. The Bible class made a desperately admirable effort to run things normally despite the inordinate attention being given them because in their midst was a man with a strong likelihood of being the next leader of the free world.

Class president Cody Timmerman, a retired railroad engineer, made a few announcements and secretary P. J. Wise took the roll. The class was asked how many had studied the day's lesson beforehand, how many had read the Bible daily that week, how many were staying for the church service to follow, and how many witnessing contacts had been made during the week. In response to the last query, only two could be determined, causing one member to comment, "We didn't do very good." Everyone was in good humor.

Except for the Southern dialect and the frequent references to Baptist this-and-that, the class could have been in any Protestant evangelical* church in a number of denominations. The men, all neatly attired, well mannered, and gracious to the hilt, referred to one another as Brother Clarence, Brother Jimmy, and so on. With the room comfortably air-conditioned, they even kept on their suit jackets throughout the class.

Everyone introduced himself (upon request), including "Sam Donaldson of Great Falls, Virginia," and someone commented that Sam needed no introduction because he could be seen regularly on TV. Jimmy's cousin Hugh Carter led in opening prayer, asking God's blessing on the class and giving thanks for the privilege of being Christian witnesses helping to further the kingdom of God. Hugh specifically prayed for Jimmy and "the great job he is about to undertake."

*Evangelical Christians can be distinguished primarily by the importance they attach to the Christian conversion experience. They believe that people are born in sin and are bound for a literal hell unless by faith they appropriate God's offer of salvation made possible by Christ's death and resurrection. Evangelicals are found in many denominations and at virtually every economic and social level.

The lesson that day, scheduled long before by Baptist curriculum publishers to fit in with the forthcoming bicentennial commemoration, was taken from Romans 13. This passage has long been one of the most controversial in the Bible with respect to how much loyalty is owed to the state and how much to God. Carter commented, "I think the news people who are not Baptists who want to know our feeling about church and state can very well take the text of the lesson." Carter later arranged to have a portion of the teacher's manual photocopied and distributed to interested newsmen.

The class used a curriculum booklet prepared by the Southern Baptist Sunday School Board based on the International Sunday School Lessons, Uniform Series. It is a system that enables churches of many different denominations to study the same part of the Bible on the same day. This particular booklet is designed for adults ages thirty through fifty-nine and uses a 1963 statement of "The Baptist Faith and Message" as a doctrinal guide.

The "golden text" or "verse to remember" that day was, "We ought to obey God rather than men" (Acts 5:39). Class members had brought their Bibles (Jimmy carried a *New Marked Reference Bible* with his name in gold on the cover) and read selected passages out loud in unison.

The point of the lesson, brought out very clearly by teacher Clarence Dodson, was that Christians have a responsibility not only to obey the state but to serve it well, the one qualification being that in the event of conflict a person is obliged to do God's will. Donaldson, of the ABC network, cornered Carter after the class and questioned him about unjust laws. Carter replied that one needs to be prepared to take the state's punishment if he or she disobeys the state.

No one gave any indication of feeling uncomfortable in the presence of Jimmy. The regulars went out of their way to make the visitors feel at home, despite the Secret Service people who hovered about the candidate. There were no searches, and no one was kept out of the church or the classroom. The only explicit restriction was the prohibition of cameras inside the building. Outside on the church grounds, film was being exposed at a rate that would have encouraged Kodak directors to declare an extra dividend.

Some newsmen attending the class had to be wondering if all this could be for real—especially in connection with a politician who had come as far as Carter. Undoubtedly, a number of other people across the country were also having a tough time believing their eyes and their ears. The setting was too quaint and too antiquated for words, incongruous when pitted against their perception of the state and spirit of the nation. How could someone still consciously and intentionally attached to this religious milieu also have the skills and insights to make it to the threshold of the political ultimate?

Yet here was a man, brought up in a supposedly secular society, who had come virtually out of nowhere to capture most of the Democratic primaries, saying more plainly than ever that he puts Jesus first in his life.

What does that mean? What is Carter talking about when he claims to be "born again"? What does an evangelical believe? And how do these religious phenomena relate to his political proposals?

"It is very difficult for anyone who has not had that experience to understand," Carter told a Baptist editor. "You do because you have had that experience. But many of the newsmen who ask about this have never had this experience. Some of them are downright cynical about it. I think it worries some of them. I just explain my own spiritual experience openly and honestly. When I first was asked this question, I had to decide how I was going to respond with the same kind of openness and honesty to this question that I would to any other question."

Primarily because of the great influence of secularism in America, the Carter "religious issue" has indeed worried not only newsmen but many others. "He can't be serious" was the thought uppermost in many American minds in the first half of 1976. Then the deduction: "This must be a cover for something sinister." Frankly, it was all too much to believe, given the day and age.

Even Carter's fellow Christians pinched themselves. Could it be true that he was really saying those things—in public, at that level? Many conservative Protestants have been praying all their lives for someone to speak up this way. Some, now that it is happening, wonder whether it is a good idea after all. From Carter's mother on down, there have been murmurs that he should not be so outspoken. Graduates at one Christian college heard their commencement speaker, a devout believer, confess, "I shudder a little bit when I hear Jimmy Carter state his Christian claims and views so publicly. I sort of wish he would keep them more to himself, and whisper them to only his closest friends."

As the initial shock wore off, however, a swell of enthusiasm emerged in that substantial part of the citizenry which regards itself as the evangelical community. Evangelist Billy Graham spoke for millions when he told newsmen, "It's a refreshing thing to have candidates come along and talk about their devotion to God, especially if they back it up with their lives." Before the primary campaign got very far along, President Gerald Ford and former California governor Ronald Reagan, vying for the Republican presidential nomination, also tested the religious waters. After Carter's spiritual experiences aroused such interest, both Ford and Reagan began addressing themselves more frequently to questions of spiritual significance. Each had previously claimed

Christian convictions closely paralleling if not coinciding with Carter's. Democratic hopeful George Wallace also was in the conservative Protestant camp. None of these men, however, ever approached the outspokenness evinced by Carter.

Despite a late start, California governor Jerry Brown got into the act with a strong showing in the primaries. Brown, once a Jesuit seminarian, distinguished himself with monkish austerity and a bent toward Eastern mysticism. He has said that "the doctrine of the Mystical Body is an idea that certainly has political implications on how people are treated, what their importance in life is."

Remarkably, none of the overtly religious candidates felt any strongly adverse reaction at the polls, at least in the heartland. They fared better on the whole than contenders who played down their faith, and Carter, the most candid Christian of all, came out ahead.

Was this coincidence, or did their successes suggest a newly discernible desire on the part of more voters for greater spiritual priorities? Did these candidates merely represent a coincidence of factors that stretched beyond what would be generally considered the strictly religious realm? Or was a broader sociological reality manifesting itself in the United States in the spring of the bicentennial year? Indeed, did the concerned citizenry signal their realization of a changing set of needs and desires that might point toward a new American consensus in ethics and values?

Some tended to dismiss the uproar as a fluke and predicted that the attention given it would quickly fade. Others thought the situation only demonstrated a vacuum, that the various candidates had not found themselves enough "solid" issues to fight about for the benefit of the constantly copy-hungry news people. How else would *religion* rate such play in the media?

Here and there, however, polls were divulging tips that a fresh look at the country from an intelligent and truly objective religious perspective might reveal an altering posture toward moral and ethical expectations, a movement toward a stricter frame of reference.

Was the national trauma of the late '60s and early '70s now being distilled into fresh and more intense political demands that were perceived to have inspired previous generations of great people? Could it be that people were starting to look in a different direction for adequate leadership, realizing that science and technology had not appeared to bestow appreciable benefits upon the democratic process? Were they saying, in the case of Carter and Brown, that they were tired of both left and right clichés and that they were seeking alignments more meaningful and promising in the context of today's special problems? Did they see old categories as too competitive with one another and woefully in need of a more transcending entity, maybe even something that we might, for lack of a more precise term, call love?

As Carter flew about the country in a three-engined Boeing 727 (chartered from United Air Lines and captained, appropriately and by design, by another James Carter), data was accumulating that would begin to shape these stirrings. Much was published and broadcast about "what makes Jimmy run," the appeal of his personality and posture, the magnetism of his smile, and the strong effects of his eyes in facc-to-face confrontations. Also considerably discussed where his organizational and managerial abilities, his indefatigable spirit, and the high degree of efficiency he achieved through his relatively young, inexperienced, and low-paid staff. What was largely overlooked was the special new mood of America that Carter found himself fitting into readily and comfortably. For all the politicians in Washington with their highly sensitive antennae, no one else was picking up to an equivalent degree the changes taking place on the broad national scene and in the composite American psyche.

Jimmy Carter represented a new hope for the pious, for the

impatient, and for those who think that America has already seen its best days unless there is a turnabout from the material to the spiritual.

Even for a Southerner, for a Baptist, and for an evangelical Christian, Carter as a politician is a rare bird. These species have always been in Washington, albeit in limited numbers, but few have dared to discuss their spiritual experiences with the media.

A comprehensive summary of the religious sentiments of past presidential candidates, contained in a book on campaign biographies by William Burlie Brown, notes a fairly consistent pattern from 1824 to 1960. "He is deeply reverent but never sanctimonious," says Brown. "Although he is an 'orthodox Christian' he is not narrowly sectarian. Above all he is tolerant—a firm believer in religious freedom. . . . In essence the principle that can be extracted from countless expressions on the subject in the campaign biographies boils down to this: religion is only a personal matter between each man and God in so far as it involves a choice of a Christian sect; but while it is important that such a choice be made, it does not matter which sect is chosen. There is no exclusive path to salvation." Carter has made a great deal more of his faith than anyone cited by Brown.

As the primaries progressed, some observers became impressed with the intensity of the religious issue. They argued as to whether the impact was positive or negative, but on the whole they agreed that the presidential race would feel it. Writing in the *Christian Century,* Kenneth Briggs, the astute religion editor of the *New York Times,* predicted that "religion potentially will play a decisive role." *Time* magazine said that "if the economy continues to improve and no foreign scares intervene, this spiritual issue could transcend all others this year."

Although the primary results did not seem to reflect discernible negative effects from the religious issue, Carter and his staff knew it could hurt him. While some evangelicals cheered him on, and others were glad to see someone stand up and be counted, there were also those who were troubled by the religious rhetoric, as it was sometimes called. In *New York* magazine Richard Reeves quoted one of the most intense reactions, attributed to an official of the Kennedy Institute of Politics at Harvard: "I would never vote for anyone who believed in God."

Part of this animosity is historic bad blood between the modern intelligensia and the Puritans from whom evangelicals derive much of their outlook. According to modern historians who are beginning to resurrect a more authentic Puritan, this early colonial group does not deserve the measure of negativity popularly attributed to them. Meanwhile, people still find it hard to relate sympathetically to various Puritan traits. We tend to feel, for example, that they were too sure of themselves, too emphatic in thinking that they were recipients of God's grace. Catherine Drinker Bowen said she attempted to write about both Jonathan Edwards and Oliver Cromwell but "could not . . . because of the Puritan cant, which comes through the letter books with a self-righteous whine."

A totally different and perhaps more serious kind of anxiety arose over Carter among some American Jews, who had also been made uneasy by such high-visibility evangelical events as the 1966 World Congress on Evangelism in Berlin and the 1974 International Congress on World Evangelization in Lausanne, Switzerland. Jews were contacted by Carter and his people all over the country in an effort to emphasize Carter's personal belief in the separation of church and state—a principle traditionally held by Baptists. "I also believe," he told Jews, "that this is a country where anyone's own religious beliefs should not be a matter of prejudice or concern . . . of all the people in the world who should have the least prejudice because of another's religious faith, it should certainly be you." Carter added that he was relying heavily on the belief that "the people of our country have an understanding and lack of prejudice." He issued a reminder that Southern Baptists are particularly proud of their local church autonomy, which means they never consider themselves subservient to ecclesiastical hierarchy. In a New Jersey appearance before the Jewish community, Carter, wearing a blue velvet yarmulke, closed his address by remarking that in 1948 when the United States became the first country to recognize the new state of Israel the president was Harry Truman, a Baptist.

Rabbi Marc H. Tanenbaum, national interreligious affairs director of the American Jewish Committee, released a statement that allayed many misgivings about Carter. Tanenbaum said it was becoming clear that the election process "is a forge for burning off our pretensions about pluralism and for enabling each major religio-ethnic group to challenge the willingness of the national society to accept its first-class citizenship *de facto* and not only *de jure*. In 1960, the Roman Catholic community in America went through that national rite of passage. In 1976, the evangelical Christian community is engaged in such a rite of passage into national acceptance."

An endorsement of Carter by U.S. Senator Abraham Ribicoff of Connecticut carried a similar tone: "All my life I have insisted that no man should be denied high public office because of his race, color, or creed. If a Catholic or a Jew, or a black should have this right, why should not a Southern Baptist have this right as well?"

Regarding Middle East issues, Carter told Jewish leaders in Los Angeles and other places, "I have never advocated withdrawal of Israel to her pre-1967 borders. I think this would not be consonant with the 1967 [United Nations] resolution that the borders have to be defensible." Carter said he would respond instantly to another oil boycott, that he would not ship the boycotting nations any food, weapons, spare parts for weapons, oil drilling rigs, or oil pipes. He also argued that "a lasting peace in the Mideast must be based on the absolute assurance of Israel's survival and security. I would never yield on that point." On another occasion Carter said: "I think the establishment of Israel. . . . is a fulfillment of biblical prophecy. I think God wants the Jews to have a place to live."

It is unfortunately true that a few people who regard themselves as Christians and even as fundamentalists or evangelicals harbor attitudes that are decidedly anti-Semitic, and there are others who fail to identify with the horrors of the holocaust. But it is also true that Jews have not found more help and encouragement in any other sector of Christendom than in the evangelical community.

Barbara Tuchman, a noted Jewish author, recorded in detail the important role British evangelicals played in the long effort to get Jews back to Palestine. Seeking to convert the Jews, evangelicals nonetheless also worked for the restoration of Israel because they believed God mandated it in the Bible.

Carter explained his positions in advertisements run in a number of Jewish papers. He pointed out that three of his closest advisers were Jewish: attorney Robert Lipshutz, national campaign treasurer; Gerald Rafshoon, the campaign media director; and Stuart Eisenstat, the campaign issues and policy director. A group of Atlanta Jewish leaders also came to Carter's defense, stating that as governor Carter appointed numerous qualified Jews to prominent positions in state government "which Jews had never before held in the history of Georgia—including judgeships and the most prestigious policy-making boards." Also noted was a special statement Carter had drawn up in support of Soviet Jewry. "He is a religious, ethical person," the group said. "But this is reason for support, not concern."

The religious issue opened up by Carter underscored to the

whole world the necessity of reckoning with religious issues more openly. Many wars can be traced in some measure to religious disputes: Jew versus Muslim versus Christian in the Middle East, Catholic versus Protestant in Ireland, Hindu versus Muslim on the Indian subcontinent. Even the war in Vietnam had a religious backdrop: A million or more Catholic refugees who fled communism in the north gained influence over the more numerous Buddhists in the south.

Political interests have always moved quickly to exploit unrest, whether caused by religious tensions or other kinds of conflicts. Religious issues, though crucial, thus get overshadowed by political ramifications. For example, Israel is not about to give up Jerusalem in exchange for any amount of oil-rich Arab real estate. The city is too significant religiously. Muslims likewise would not yield their claims on the Holy City for any price.

The world desperately needs to find formulas by which peoples can live together without compromising fundamental religious beliefs.

The political elite, usually only vaguely religious if at all, have tended to make light of the zeal with which religious beliefs are held and to bypass the adequate discussion of them in public forums. Alongside the argument that religion is or ought to be a private matter has been the fear that religion is a powerful force and that giving attention to it will set uncontrollable power in motion. As a result, sensitizing responsible world opinion to religion-related dangers is difficult. For years after the U.N. Commission on Human Rights introduced a declaration against religious intolerance, action was delayed. Neither East nor West expressed much concern over the foot dragging.

The perils of such neglect in the United States were pointed out by Elwyn A. Smith, author of *Religious Liberty in the United States,* an exhaustive and scholarly work not given to rash statements: "Since church-state debate moved substantially into the courts, a range of problems has appeared that was not previously apparent. The inherent difficulty of achieving a stabilization of church-state relations in a pluralistic society is clearer than ever. Regulation of disputes in such a way as to suppress damaging conflict and defend civil and religious liberty is a fully sufficient expectation. A failure of judicial wisdom could remove church-state dispute from the courtroom to the less disciplined forum of socially destructive partisanship and conflict."

The whole world stands to benefit by greater candor with respect to religion. Bringing faith into the open, as Carter has done, is what evangelicals want and perhaps what most of the rest of the citizenry wants as well. Refusing to talk about what we hold dear only increases the chances of conflict over it.

There is a lot of resistance to the Christian message in the modern world because it is considered too restrictive of thought and action. The Christian's answer is that the message is actually liberating because its essence deals more effectively than anything in this world with the debilitating effects of evil. God, moreover, leaves a great deal for individuals to decide for themselves through their consciences. A key norm is whether one heeds his or her conscience or acts in pragmatic self-interest, often considered the usual route for politicians.

Jim Newton, editor of the *World Mission Journal* of the Southern Baptist Convention Brotherhood Commission (of which Carter is a trustee), asked Carter how he would use the office of president, if elected, to demonstrate his Christian convictions.

"I would try to exemplify in every moment of my life those attitudes and actions of Christianity that I believe in," Carter replied. "I would ask God for guidance on decisions affecting our country and make those decisions after evaluating the alternatives as best I could. I would recognize that my influence on others would be magnified 100 times over as President. . . . Because I am a Christian, I feel my limitations more intensely. I used to deny my limitations and conceal them. Now I am much easier in my relations with other people and with God."

Carter's spiritual pilgrimage began in a rather formal way. His account of it in *Christian Life* magazine said merely that "I had accepted Jesus into my heart when a young boy of 11 years. . . . I recited the necessary steps of acknowledging my sinfulness, of repentance and asking Jesus to enter into my heart and life as Lord and Savior." He then went on to tell of the new commitment he made in adulthood.

Young Carter's start on the Christian journey was signified in the traditional Baptist manner. He was baptized by immersion.* His baptism, his mother says, took place on a Sunday evening after he had responded to the plea of a visiting evangelist during a series of revival services which had extended through the previous week.

Immersion is not a belief peculiar to Baptists. Many Protestant churches feel that "sprinkling" children does not adequately implement the scriptural requirement. Some Christians place even greater importance on its necessity than do Baptists, and Protestants have long argued over the relation of baptism to conversion. G. W. Grogan summarizes the issue well in an article in *The New International Dictionary of the Christian Church:* "Evangelicals see baptism as the sign and seal of regeneration while Roman Catholics see it also as conveying the regenerating grace it signifies."

In Southern Baptist churches more than in other evangelical

*Churches which practice this kind of baptism usually have a baptistery behind the altar for this purpose. It is in effect an oversized bathtub which is filled waist deep. It must be large enough for a clergyman and a baptismal candidate to stand in together. The clergyman actually puts the candidate completely under for a moment. Ponds and streams are still sometimes used as well. Many a recent baptism has been conducted in swimming pools of private homes.

congregations there is considerable encouragement to enter church membership at the time of the initial profession of faith. Jimmy's name was therefore added to the rolls of the Baptist church in Plains, Georgia, which he and his parents attended.

In traditional Southern Baptist practice the pastor issues an appeal at the close of the sermon before the benediction is pronounced. People are invited to step out of their pews and stand in front of the church to indicate publicly their commitment to Christ, and this action is taken also to signify their desire to be baptized and to join the church as official members (Roman Catholics also associate baptism and church membership but in their case the rites are held at the initiative of parents and the infants are sprinkled, not immersed). Other evangelical churches tend to separate commitment, baptism, and church membership to the extent that years may elapse between the times a person chooses to take the various steps.

Baptismal services normally are announced in advance in all churches. Carter has noted that in racially segregated churches such as the one he attended in Plains baptisms, weddings, and funerals were special occasions. Both white and black people were welcome to attend these events. Carter, who actually grew up more than a mile west of the town of Plains in an unincorporated community known as Archery, recalls that "the most important event which ever occurred" there was the funeral of an African Methodist Episcopal bishop. That was in 1936 when Carter was twelve. Preachers, choirs, and mourners came from long distances. Dozens of white friends attended the service in the AME church in Archery, where the bishop had lived and ministered. Forty years later Carter addressed the quadrennial convention of the AME denomination, one of the largest of the American black community, in Atlanta as the heir apparent of the Democratic presidential nomination.

In addition to his religious upbringing, Carter's cultural educa tion was rare for someone in a rural situation. For the latter Carter is thankful to the late Julia Coleman, the local school superintendent who made a great impression on young Carter. She was strict with the children she taught, and in the years Carter was a pupil, the students respected her.

"She was short and somewhat crippled," Carter says in his autobiography, "yet she was quite graceful as she moved along. Her face was expressive, particularly when she was reading one of the poems she loved, or presenting to a class the paintings of Millet, Gainsborough, Whistler, or Sir Joshua Reynolds."

Carter told Bill Moyers in a television interview that Julia Coleman made sure he listened to classical music. "She would make me do it," he said. "And she'd make sure that I learned the famous paintings, and the author, and the artists, and she gave me lists of books to read."

When he was about twelve, she called him in and introduced him to Tolstoy's *War and Peace.* Even though it did not turn out to be about cowboys, which was Carter's first impression, it did prove to be one of his favorite books. As a classic account of Napoleon's epic and ultimately unsuccessful struggle against Russia, *War and Peace* instilled into Carter a bent toward what in America in the 1970s would be regarded as an appeal through populism.

Arthur Schlesinger, Jr., has suggested that Carter is theologically fuzzy in admiring both Tolstoy and Reinhold Niebuhr. But E. Brooks Holifield, professor of American religious history at Emory University, disagrees. "Carter was not taken with Tolstoy's pacifism or his religious ethics," Holifield wrote in the *New Republic.* "He was impressed, rather, with Tolstoy's insistence in *War and Peace* that the course of history is determined not by powerful, competent and ruthless leaders (not even by generals) but by the inclinations, passions, will power, courage, prejudices and inarticulate aspirations of the masses. Niebuhr would not have been uncomfortable with that notion."

James Earl Carter, Jr., was an only son until his teens, but had two sisters by then: Gloria, two years younger, and Ruth, three years his junior. A brother, Billy, was born when Jimmy was thirteen.

Carter's father affectionately referred to Jimmy as "Hot," as in "Hot Shot." Mr. Carter was a good athlete and, according to Jimmy, an exceptional tennis player. There was a tennis court on the farm, and three other courts were located in Plains.

Life in Archery and Plains was revolutionized when electricity was introduced through the Rural Electrification Program. The agency, established by President Roosevelt in 1935 by executive order and given legislative undergirding by Congress the following year, lent money for construction of power lines in rural areas In 1936 only one of every ten farms had electricity.

Carter's rural roots gave him a permanent affinity to the soil, but his environment and upbringing added a dimension to his life from the cultural and technological spheres. He absorbed the various aspects of his background into his personality in a way that produced a winning combination.

Carter says he had his first date when he was thirteen. At the time he was spending Friday evenings at the home of his paternal grandmother in Plains, where young people assembled each week for street games. Jimmy got to know his classmates better that way. The girl he initially went out with lived next door to his grandmother. For the date he was also out on his own for the first time with the family pickup truck.

Carter did not begin courting the hometown girl who became his wife until the summer before his last year at Annapolis.

Almost as long as he can remember, Carter had his heart set on going to the U.S. Naval Academy, partly because his mother's youngest brother had been a career man in the navy, and his travels around the world aboard ship had aroused hero worship in Jimmy. Uncle Tom nourished Jimmy's interest and admiration by sending back mementos of his visits to various ports. The uncle was further etched into Jimmy's memory when Tom was taken prisoner by the Japanese on Guam at the outset of World War II and the Red Cross sent notification of his death. Tom's wife remarried only to learn after the war that he had been found alive in Japan. The two were never reconciled.

Young Carter also dreamed of going to Annapolis because during the depression any other way of getting a college education seemed financially out of the question. He did get his appointment, but between high-school graduation and enrollment at the Naval Academy Carter also attended a small junior college and was registered at Georgia Tech in the navy ROTC program.

Writing in *Atlanta* magazine long afterward, Carter said of Annapolis, "I got only $4 a month when I first got there, and later $7 a month, and I spent all of it on records. I knew every note of every Rachmaninoff concerto and every Wagner opera. I could even compare piano techniques."

While attending the Naval Academy, Carter began teaching a Sunday school class of girls aged nine through eleven at a Baptist church in Annapolis, a town on the western side of the Chesapeake Bay originally settled by Puritans in 1649. Following graduation he taught a Sunday school class of fellow crew members on board ship. Once while out at sea on a submarine he conducted Easter services in the torpedo room.

Such attention to perpetuating church teaching attracted great attention for Carter from fellow Christians in 1976, but it created special demands upon him as well. Could he demonstrate that he is not just using the appeal of religion to the masses?

Carter frequently quotes Niebuhr's maxim that "the sad duty

of politics is to establish justice in a sinful world." He also cites Niebuhr's premise that laws are constantly changing to stabilize the social balance of the competing forces of a dynamic society. But as Holifield points out, Carter stands in a long line of politicians who began to appreciate Niebuhr after becoming involved in the complexities of power. "His [Carter's] evangelical tradition did not provide a language for dealing with such realities," Holifield argued. "Carter's acquaintance with Niebuhr dates back at least to the early '60s, when he and William Gunter, now an associate justice of the Georgia Supreme Court, began having periodic informal discussions about theology. Gunter gave Carter a copy of *Reinhold Niebuhr on Politics,* a compilation of lengthy excerpts that became, in Gunter's words, 'a political Bible' for Carter. After reading Niebuhr the two men agreed that 'love and kindness meant a great deal in one-to-one relationships but not in dealings with structures and corporate groups.' "

Reinhold Niebuhr, a native of Missouri, was probably the most influential theoretician produced by the twentieth century in the field of Christian social ethics. He grew up in a church which became part of what is now called the United Church of Christ. After graduate study at Eden Theological Seminary and Yale Divinity School, he became pastor of a church in Detroit. There he thought long and hard about the problems of urban life in an industrial society. In 1928 he became a professor at Union Theological Seminary in New York and taught there for thirty-two years.

Niebuhr is quoted by modern politicians more than any other thinker, not so much because his answers to problems are attractive, but because he obviously grappled more profoundly with them. He was one of the greatest names in the theological movement called *neo-orthodoxy.* This term covers a broad area but basically represents a conservative turn from classic theological liberalism which reflected a highly optimistic view of man as a creature who is constantly getting better and better. The two world wars are generally credited with putting an end to classic liberalism as a major force in the theological world. Neo-orthodoxy, which replaced it, took the Bible more literally and more seriously but never moved completely to a position in which evangelicals and fundamentalists would be comfortable. There was a great deal of disagreement and rivalry between major figures in neo-orthodoxy, Niebuhr often attacking the leading theologian of the movement, Karl Barth, on grounds that Barth was too abstract.

Neo-orthodoxy is not be to confused with neo-evangelicalism, more an ecclesiastical rather than a theological term. Barth took sharp issue with liberalism's stress upon the immanence of God, that is, the immediate presence of God in the affairs of men, as over against transcendence, the idea that there is an apartness in God's nature and that we cannot consider everything that happens on earth as directly the work of God. In a way, transcendence is an attempt to explain the presence of evil without reducing the concept of God's sovereignty over his creation.

Neo-evangelicalism is something else. Harold John Ockenga, who is most commonly regarded as the patron-prophet of the movement, describes it in a foreword to *The Battle for the Bible* by Harold Lindsell. Says Ockenga, "It differed from neo-orthodoxy in its emphasis upon the written word as inerrant over against the Word of God which was above and different from the scripture, but was manifested in scripture. It differed from fundamentalism in its repudiation of separatism and its determination to engage itself in the theological dialogue of the day. It had a new emphasis upon the application of the Gospel to the sociological, political, and economic areas of life."

Niebuhr started out as quite an idealist. In 1930, as a Socialist, he ran unsuccessfully for Congress. As late as 1935 he was saying that on the whole "it must be admitted that rationalistic political theory from Aristotle and the Stoics to the thought of the eighteenth century and, the theories of Marx, have contributed more to a progressive reassessment of the problems of justice with which politics deals" than either orthodox or liberal Christian thought. He did acknowledge as exceptions the contribution of Thomistic Catholicism to the peace and order of thirteenth century Europe and the "dynamic relation of Calvinism to the democratic developments" of the seventeenth and eighteenth centuries. "Among the many possible causes of this failure of Christianity in politics," Niebuhr said, "the most basic is the tendency of Christianity to destroy the dialectic of prophetic religion, either by sacrificing time and history to eternity or by giving ultimate significance to the relativities of history. Christian orthodoxy chose the first alternative, and Christian liberalism the second. The problems of politics were confused by the undue pessimism of the orthodox church and the undue sentimentality of the liberal church. In the one case the fact of the single 'sinfulness of the world' was used as an excuse for the complacent acceptance of whatever imperfect justice a given social order had established. . . . In the other case the problems of politics were approached from a perspective of the sentimental moralism with no understanding for either the mechanistic and amoral factors in social life or the mechanical and technical prerequisites of social justice."

Niebuhr's major contribution was to introduce a pragmatism and an existential element. It is difficult to deduce from Niebuhr's thought that he believed in thus-and-so particular political principles. There is an abstract quality about him not unlike that which he criticized in Barth. The basic conclusion was put well by Holifield, that Niebuhr felt "a realistic goal for Christians was not the establishment of a loving society but rather a relatively just order maintained through a balance of forces."

Niebuhr did take sides in specific situations and was behind the founding of the journal *Christianity and Crisis* in 1941. That was partly because the distinguished journal the *Christian Century*, for decades the most influential periodical in American Protestantism, had been inclined toward pacifism.

An interesting historical twist is that in 1976 Jimmy Carter continued to quote Niebuhr respectfully even while counting on the editor of the *Century*, James M. Wall, to play an important role in the primary campaign. Wall, a United Methodist clergyman and a native of Georgia who had known Carter personally less than a year, served as the contender's campaign chairman for the Illinois Democratic primary—as an unpaid volunteer. By this time, of course, the *Century* as a magazine had gone through an evolution which took it far from espousal of the old liberalism. Also considerably diminished were the earlier attacks on fundamentalists and evangelicals.

Wall, a political liberal who had run unsuccessfully for Congress, said he had deep respect for Carter's religious conservatism and decided to support him vigorously because Carter had convinced Wall of his good character and ability to govern. Wall apparently had some abilities of his own along political lines because Carter won the Illinois primary decisively. Carter's victory there coupled with a defeat of George Wallace in the Florida primary the previous week seemed to avenge the earlier loss in Massachusetts and put him in the driver's seat.

Although familiarity with Niebuhr's thought could not help but instill in a person a greater sense of Christian responsibility in the social sphere, Carter made many enemies among fundamentalists for his ideological kinship with Niebuhr. Even a number of Carter's fellow Southern Baptists fail to distinguish between a variety of "modernists." Evangelicals (they are only called neo-evangelicals when it is necessary to distinguish them from traditional fundamentalists) are concerned about Niebuhr's view of the Bible as are the more conservative Christians, but many see a great deal of value in Niebuhr's work.

One aspect of the religious issue regarding Carter was concern about *his* view of the Bible, especially after *Time* magazine quoted him as saying, "I find it difficult to question Holy Scripture, but I admit I do have trouble with Paul sometimes, especially when he says that a woman's place is with her husband, and that she should keep quiet and should cover her head in church. I just can't go along with him on that."

At one news conference, Carter was confronted with a related question: "Governor, you've been described as a fundamental Baptist. That means you take everything in the Bible quite literally. Possibly you believe that the whale swallowed Jonah. Is that a fair characterization?" Carter replied that he respectfully retained the right to make his own analyses but added, "I don't believe everything in the Bible to be literally true. I don't think the earth was created in seven days as we know days now and I reserve the right to make my own interpretation." Popular misconceptions of the evangelical view of the Bible often focus on how literally the message is taken; evangelicals do *not* take the Bible literally when the passage in question is clearly not meant to be taken literally. They assert that the Scriptures are to be taken literally to the extent that one is to believe and obey what they purport to say. Evangelicals concede that there are parts of the Bible difficult to understand and reconcile. But they also keep in mind that to deny what God himself has said to be true and what he has attested—in ways that conscientious students of the Bible find remarkable—presents a greater problem.*

*The sole criterion for membership in the Evangelical Theological Society has been to affirm, "The Bible alone, and the Bible in its entirety, is the word of God written, and therefore inerrant in the autographs."

The easy way out of religious issues is to dodge them in one's life, and a large segment of the American people are saying in 1976 that they are tired of that route. They are also saying that they have had enough of cynicism and double-dealing, these facets of the American psyche having at times approached the status of a civil religion.

At the center of the new mood are the evangelicals, suddenly being regarded as the most understated demographical reality in the whole nation if not as the most identifiable theological consensus. An official of the National Council of Churches has been raising many eyebrows with his candid book *Why Conservative Churches Are Growing.*

The appeal of someone like Jimmy Carter with his candid style and forthright convictions is therefore obvious. Occasionally, however, Carter implies the essential goodness of all people or makes a statement from which such a meaning could readily be inferred. For evangelicals that outlook represents an avenue that needs to be looked into more thoroughly. One evangelical reviewer of Carter's autobiography asked whether the premise was biblical. Said Stephen Noll in the *National Courier,* "The Bible says that everyone has gone astray, each one to his own way, and that when God does call a true leader he is often unpopular and even persecuted for the truth."

2

From Plains, Georgia . . .

So QUICKLY did Jimmy Carter rise to national prominence that millions of Americans tabbed him their next president before millions of their fellow citizens could recognize his name. Historians will collect the reasons for and speculate upon his success for decades to come, but psychologists may be inclined to explain it largely in terms of his ability to identify with people quite different from himself without repudiating his own background.

Carter's capacity to relate to ethnic groups became apparent during the primary campaign. After seeing Carter at a gospel music concert in an Indianapolis black church, William Lee Miller wrote in the *Washington Post*, "Neither Ike nor Jerry Ford nor Ronald Reagan nor any other national politician of recent memory, if he came to this church, could ever, ever, ever, ever, ever, ever (to lapse into the rhythm of the music) have made himself at one with the congregation as Carter was to do."

People whose upbringing and outlook are different from Carter's sense his empathy and then are encouraged to give a little toward his side. Such adaptation was evident during a primary rally Carter attended in Cincinnati. It was also a black gathering with a piano-drum-guitar trio providing the entertainment. Out of deference to the occasion they played but one number, repeating over and over in rock beat and tempo several measures from "The Stars and Stripes Forever."

But in going up and down the land Carter has been careful not to sever his roots. He says his favorite book is James Agee's *Let Us Now Praise Famous Men,* a report on sharecropper life. He gives as his favorite hymn (actually a gospel song) "Amazing Grace," long loved by Southern church people and evangelicals everywhere. The words were written by John Newton, who experienced a remarkable conversion after a life of debauchery and destitution. The phrase "servant of slaves" appears on his tombstone in Olney, England, and is also the title of a highly acclaimed novel by Grace Irwin based on Newton's life.

Carter not only kept in touch with the people who were in his past but stayed with them as much as possible even after going into politics at the state level and after entering the primaries. As much of the world now knows, he is a resident of Plains, Georgia. He talks about Plains a great deal in his travels and frequently reminisces. During the primaries he made it a point to come home as often as possible, usually on weekends, and to worship in his own church on Sunday mornings. He determined to keep teaching an occasional Sunday school class. The trips to Plains, regular even through the most hectic phases of the campaign, reflected the candidate's priorities. They increased travel costs, but they kept him in touch with a valuable heritage and retained for him the respect of people who identified with it. In 1976 Carter even managed to participate in an Easter sunrise service at the Plains Baptist Church.

Carter told a reunion of his high-school class in 1976, "I want to be close to you . . . I always want to make you proud of me." There were indications that Carter would try to keep his Plains ties a means to offset temptations to get carried away with new-found political power and to become preoccupied with the high and mighty to such an extent that identification with grass-roots realities is lost. Shortly after delivering his speech accepting the Democratic presidential nomination, Carter told a reporter that people could not really understand him unless they knew about Plains, and he added that he determined to keep returning to Plains. That contact, he said, serves as a stabilizing influence in his life.

Indirectly, Carter aims to recover some respectability for the redneck, the Southern rural white worker often regarded as a bigot. Carter does not condone evil, but he does contend that lower- and middle-class people are similar throughout America and should not be at each other's throats. All have inadequacies, and it is up to their leaders to bring out the best in them.

Carter wrote in *Atlanta* magazine, "I do believe that being from a rural community has helped me politically and has given me the assurance that there is no inherent difference between the problems (and opportunities) of urban and rural Georgians." After campaigning throughout the country and getting to know people from all walks of life, Carter's wife observed that the primary lesson of those experiences was that human beings everywhere have the same basic concerns.

Perhaps the most dramatic innovations proposed by Carter as a presidential candidate actually stem from his instincts as an agriculturalist. He talks about management, goals, planning, and efficiency that can be measured. Those seem like platitudes until one stops to consider that they represent a different kind of rhetoric for presidential campaigns. Management theory has been around a long time and has gone through various evolutions, and government agencies have achieved some implementation but not on any coordinated basis that would embrace all of the executive branch. Carter argues for a hardheaded business approach starting at the top, and he was much influenced on the need for it by his farmer orientation. The successful farmer operating in unchangeable yearly cycles on a given segment of acreage is disciplined to use management techniques whether he recognizes them as such or not. Failure to follow predetermined objectives on schedule is the sure route to financial loss.

Before Carter put it on the map, Plains had a population of 683, having neither grown nor declined appreciably for decades. The town lies in the southwestern part of Georgia about fifty miles southeast of Columbus, where the mammoth Fort Benning army base is located and where the Chattahoochee River separates Georgia and Alabama. When Carter was born near Plains on October 1, 1924, the town straddled a dirt road. Now the main road is U.S. Highway 280, connecting Columbus with Savannah on the Atlantic Ocean more than two hundred miles away.

Plains is within one hundred fifty miles or so of the Gulf of Mexico, a factor in the area climate. An average January day has a low temperature in the forties and a high reading in the sixties. Snow is rare.

At Warm Springs, Georgia, not far from Columbus, an institution was established for the treatment of polio using water that always comes out of the ground at a temperature of eighty-eight degrees. Franklin Delano Roosevelt, having suffered from polio, often stayed at a "Little White House" in Warm Springs. He died there in 1945 in his fourth term as president. Since then, Warm Springs has been the main tourist attraction in the area. In 1976, however, Plains is diverting considerable attention from Warm Springs.

The Carter primary campaign had no slogan, but the peanut

took on a symbolism for the candidate because it is the most important crop in the area around Plains. About twelve thousand tons of peanuts are said to be marketed there each season. Peanuts are not true botanical nuts but rather the legume of *Arachis hypogaea* in the pea family. They have the peculiar habit of ripening in the ground even though the plant blossoms above ground like any other. It is a misnomer to apply the term *peanuts* to something of little worth because peanuts, despite their relatively low price in an inflationary period, are an unusually valuable commodity. The peanut is a highly concentrated food. Doctors constantly tell parents to quit worrying about their children's binges of peanut-butter sandwiches. By weight, peanuts contain more protein, minerals, and vitamins than beef liver, more fat than heavy cream, and more food energy than sugar. More than a million tons of peanuts are grown in the United States each year, and most are used for food although oil is an important byproduct.

The progress of Carter's campaign reminded some observers of the question attributed to God in the Book of Zechariah, "Who has despised the day of small things?" (Zech. 4:10). Carter's first obstacle as a candidate was to endure taunts ranging from "Jimmy who?" to "Running for what?" As time went on it became obvious that like the peanut the campaign was going to amount to something quite beyond first impressions. By June 1976 Carter was a household word, and peanuts had their best press since George Washington Carver discovered more than three hundred product uses for them.

Carter crusades not only for responsible agricultural policies as a result of his childhood environment but for preventive medicine. His mother, Lillian Gordy Carter, worked as a registered nurse while he was growing up, sometimes for twenty hours a day for a total of six dollars. In effect, she served as the community doctor. Apparently she took good care of herself as well as others because she was strong enough in her late sixties to do a two-year stint with the Peace Corps in India. According to Carter, her father, Jim Jack Gordy, had a claim to fame in that he conceived the idea of the rural free delivery of mail and prevailed on his congressman to implement it through federal legislation. Gordy was postmaster of a town near Plains.

Carter's father, James, Sr., doubled as a peanut farmer and storekeeper. He stood about five feet eight inches tall, about the same as the mature Jimmy, but weighed 175 pounds, somewhat more than the son, whose extraordinary energy output has undoubtedly helped keep him trim. The father served as chairman of the school board and was elected to the state legislature not long before he died. "I came home from the Navy to see my Daddy die," Carter said in *Atlanta,* "and the thought struck me that here were my roots, here were my ancestors, these were the fields I had worked in, these are the people I grew up with. . . . I felt that my Daddy's life meant more, in the long run, than mine had meant, so I got out of the Navy."

Carter remembers that his home community of Archery, outside Plains, had about two permanent white families, one or two transient white families, and about twenty-five black families. The center of the community was a Seaboard Coast Line Railroad train stop, a tiny store, a school, and the AME church. The Carters lived in a wooden clapboard farmhouse heated in winter by fireplaces with two double chimneys and by a wood stove in the kitchen.

The practice of modern management requires a strong sense of personal discipline which Carter acquired in his youth. "I never even considered disobeying my father," Carter wrote in his autobiography, "and he seldom if ever ordered me to perform a task; he simply suggested that it needed to be done, and he expected me to do it. But he was a stern disciplinarian and punished me severely when I misbehaved. From the time I was four years old until I was fifteen years old he whipped me six times and I've never forgotten any of those impressive experiences." He added that his most vivid memory of a whipping was when he was four or five. The "board of education" that was applied to the "seat of learning" was a peach tree switch. In this case the infraction had been that he took a penny out of the church offering plate instead of putting one in. "That was the last money I ever stole," Carter wrote.

The church the Carters attended is the same one they belong to now in Plains. Built in 1906, it has had a membership of about three hundred, the largest church in town. The white frame structure features gothic stained-glass windows and a steeple. Inside, the sanctuary is laid out in the form of a cross. Ornate dark pews are installed over rich maroon wall-to-wall carpeting. While Carter was trying to get nominated for the American presidency, the church was electing deacons. A sign described the qualifications: reverent, purpose in life, sound convictions, proved, dedicated, blameless, growing in faith.

There is also a Methodist church in Plains, where Jimmy and his wife were married in 1946. She had been a member of the Methodist congregation, whose present building dates back to 1910.

Located across the street from the Baptist church is a Lutheran church erected in 1907. In addition, Plains has two black churches. Together, these five congregations form an influential aspect of town life in a number of ways.

At home Jimmy's playmates were black youngsters, and his classmates at school and his friends at church were white. His best friend during childhood, A. D. Davis, was black. Davis now has a large family and works at a sawmill.

In a *New York Times Magazine* article Patrick Anderson observed: "As a boy, Carter saw his parents' differing philosophies on the race issue acted out most dramatically. Carter grew up with the crazy quilt of small-town segregation: In Archery, almost all his playmates were black, but in school or church in Plains all his classmates were white." Carter's mother was well known for her intolerance of racial segregation and recalls hearing the epithet "nigger-lover" hurled at her many times although she was never subjected to any significant abuse. Anderson, who later became a Carter speech writer, commented, "Eccentricity is a major art form of the rural South; much is forgiven anyone who breaks the monotony."

Mrs. Carter's effect upon her son became clear in his mature years when he took courageous stands against racial discrimination in his church, in his community, and in public life. He tried to work for blacks, however, without repudiating his friendships with white people who opposed him. His objective was justice mediated through the spirit of reconciliation.

In area, the town of Plains is a perfect circle with a diameter of more than a mile. The circle is roughly bisected by U.S. 280 and by tracks of the Seaboard Coast Line Railroad. By and large, whites live on the north side of the tracks, and blacks (who represent more than half the population) on the south. When segregated public schools were outlawed by the U.S. Supreme Court and civil rights activists started to demonstrate, southern whites who favored the status quo began to organize white citizens' councils. Carter refused to join, even when invited to do so by a Baptist preacher and a police chief. He and his wife found it all upsetting and thought about leaving town. The organizers offered to pay his dues, and when Carter refused that proposal also, they threatened to boycott his business.

"I've got $5," Carter has been quoted as telling them, "and I'd flush it down the toilet before I'd give it to you."

The boycott never amounted to much, according to Carter,

who always wondered thereafter what happened to the dues money the white citizens' councils extracted from people during those years. Carter had taken a stand for racial equality when still in the navy. While visiting Nassau, the crew of his submarine was invited to a party by British officials who sent a message at the last minute that it was for whites only. The Carter crew, which included a popular black sailor, stayed away in protest.

Carter regarded the racial problem in the churches of Plains as serious. He had been elected a deacon, and during a meeting he missed, the eleven other deacons voted with the pastor unanimously to bar any blacks who might show up for a service. Disturbed, Carter made it a point to get to the next monthly church conference and urged from the floor that the deacons' decision be reversed. Only one other member of the congregation voted with the Carter family to admit blacks. About fifty voted to support the deacons. Dozens abstained. One of Carter's sisters reportedly left the church membership in protest of the prohibition, but Carter remained.

Carter was already a state senator, and he was concerned about the effects of the controversy. But he later concluded that the really fervent segregationists were few in number both in Plains and in the South as a whole. The hassle over integrated public education eventually subsided when private schools were set up and expanded to accommodate the children of unyielding parents. "Perhaps these private schools were not without value in a difficult time, serving in a way as community safety valves," Carter said.

In June 1976 the "safety valves" likewise were knocked down by the U.S. Supreme Court. The effect was not expected to be immediately significant, however, because private segregated schools could still keep out most blacks by charging high tuition rates.

Carter started in public service by winning appointment to the

Sumter County library board and to the hospital authority. He also became chairman of the local planning commission, president of the Georgia Planning Association, district governor of Lions International, and state president of the Certified Seed Organization. After being named to the school board, Carter immersed himself in the problems and challenges of education. He got a taste of politicking by traveling around the county in behalf of a school-consolidation proposal which, much to his disappointment, was defeated by a narrow margin in a referendum. Some voters apparently feared that the move would encourage racially integrated schools.

A change in the method of legislative representation in Georgia prompted Carter to run for the state senate. Again he lost by a few votes. But in the process of the primary he discovered some fraudulent voting practices in a small town and began a long series of appeals. The state Democratic executive committee finally declared him the nominee, and he won the general election. His battle had the help of some exposé articles by John Pennington of the *Atlanta Journal.* Other media closer to the scene dismissed Carter as a poor loser.

Carter began the first of two terms in the Georgia senate in January 1963. He proved to be a conscientious lawmaker, making it a point to go to the capitol early every morning and vowing to read every bill before voting on it. He attracted considerable attention in work on a new state constitution, especially in his stand for freedom of religion. Carter favored the language of the U.S. Constitution while others called for a more theistic clause. Some Carter opponents thought that was "proof" he was an atheist.

As a Southern Baptist, Carter comes naturally by his stand for religious liberty. The modern Baptist movement had its start in seventeenth-century England among Christians who opposed the established church. In the nineteenth and twentieth centuries the movement has flourished in America far more than anywhere else. Baptists in America count as their greatest historical hero Roger Williams, who founded Rhode Island and in 1639 was instrumental in establishing a church there. Williams, who had been banished by Puritans from their territory, bought land from the Indians and made it a haven for all whose religious convictions set them at odds with colonial authorities.

"Roger Williams was the most beloved of colonial founders prior to William Penn," wrote historian Samuel Eliot Morison. "The Indians, whose language he studied, lodging with them 'in their filthy, smoky holes,' adored Williams because he respected their individuality, protected them against land-hungry members of his race, and never tried to convert them unless they asked for it."

Throughout the years since then, Baptists in America have championed religious liberty. A number of key Southern Baptists have been actively engaged in the work of Americans United for Separation of Church and State. Given their tradition, Baptists have a hard time understanding why anyone would think they might seek to impose their spiritual views on non-Baptists. Carter had been urged by some to select a Roman Catholic running mate to help alleviate such anxiety in the presidential election.

There is a problem, however, when one tries to think in terms of the church's role in society. On the one hand is a feeling that the church should not influence others. On the other hand, the unchurched sometimes criticize churches for dragging their feet on moral issues and for failing to exert adequate force for change. This came up quite pointedly during the days of the civil rights movement. The disgrace of keeping blacks out of sanctuaries and classrooms was appalling, but certainly the indifference of so many toward the question was itself lamentable. Partly as a result of the belated recognition of this wrong, more evangelicals began to assess conscientiously the role of their faith in the workaday world. Several eloquent young black evangelical leaders such as Howard Jones and Tom Skinner helped whites in theologically conservative churches to get a better insight into the problem. Jones has been an associate of Billy Graham, and Skinner, also an evangelist, has served for several years as chaplain for the Washington Redskins professional football team.

Evangelicals opposed the so-called Social Gospel, sometimes resisting as well what should be distinguished from it, namely, the need to allow Christ to be Lord of all one's life. Social Gospel origins date back into the nineteenth century and are associated with pastor-professor Walter Rauschenbusch, a Baptist from Rochester, New York. For more than ten years Rauschenbusch pastored a church in New York City and became a champion of socially and economically disadvantaged peoples. Theological conservatives felt he put too much stock in the perfectibility of man's institutions and was too swayed by Darwinian euphoria.

The Social Gospel movement unfortunately aroused reactions which tended to make religion into a private affair. When the twentieth-century ecumenical movement drifted into preoccupation with social concerns, it also provoked opponents into unwarranted minimization of Christian cooperative efforts. With time, evangelicals gained a more accurate perspective and grew to realize that if one is a Christian people will know it because he or she behaves differently. Evangelicals believe that God has a plan for each life and that insofar as possible ethical and moral goals should be set accordingly. Implementation of these goals cannot help but affect other people, hopefully for good. *Christian Herald* magazine told of a bulletin board outside a church in Canton, Ohio, reading, "If your religion hasn't changed you, you better change religions."

Much controversy developed in the '50s and '60s over whether churches as churches should take stands on matters of social import. Evangelicals generally criticized such actions because they bent invariably to the ideological left and because they gave the impression that the positions taken reflected a consensus of the constituency and a biblical, theological undergirding. In practice, pronouncements were normally drawn up by denominational officials desiring to reflect a prophetic voice without much reference either to opinions held at the level of the rank and file or to scriptural precedents. Seldom was the laity consulted, even when the issues involved complicated technical matters with moral implications. Tensions rose as people in the pews complained that the problems seemed to have more than one answer that could be theologically justified.

Gradually, lay persons, particularly those of evangelical persuasion, on their own began to think through Christian commitments in the context of life-work. They sought increasingly to confront social problems without lowering priorities related to regeneration. Issues related to ecology provided the biggest prod. In no small sense did this rethinking process figure in the evangelical identification with Carter as a candidate around the country. He was doing with his faith what they thought ought to be done: giving civil responsibilitics their rightful place on the spiritual agenda.

Carter frequently tells about a sermon he once heard which asked, "If you were arrested for being a Christian, would there be enough evidence to convict you?" He decided that even though he was quite active and influential in his church at that time he could probably have talked his way out of the situation!

Carter also mentions often an opportunity he once had to speak to a group in a neighboring community on the subject of "Christian Witnessing." It got him to thinking about how many visits he had made on behalf of the church, and he estimated 140 people contacted in 14 years. The total was puny in comparison to the number of citizens he had confronted in his political appeals for votes. Carter says that then and there he began to take much more seriously the Bible's admonitions about pride and self-satisfaction. "I began to expand my personal service in the church," he says, "and to search more diligently for a closer relationship with God among my different business, professional and political interests."

There is no easy resolution of the dispute as to how much the church should be involved in taking sides on social issues. Most evangelicals feel that it is not the purpose of the church to lobby for or against particular proposals or individuals. But on whether Christians should be personally involved, there is no question in the minds of most thinking evangelicals. One of the most influential events in the evangelical community in recent years was the 1969 U.S. Congress on Evangelism in Minneapolis, where a host of speakers, including Ralph Abernathy, stressed the need of identifying with victims of injustice as a precondition for effective evangelism.

Church stands on social issues are sensitive matters partly because they have historically been the cause for serious division. Baptists in the South trace their origins and initial growth to eighteenth-century revivals. But slavery was the foremost precipitating cause of the actual formation of the Southern Baptist Convention in 1845. Under pressure from abolitionists, a large group of churches pulled out of a national association of Baptists and started their own with about 350,000 members. In the first several decades growth was not remarkable, but in the twentieth century the Southern Baptist Convention has flourished. In the 1960s churches associated with the convention passed the ten-million mark in membership and became the largest Protestant denomination in America. There are now "Southern" Baptist churches in all states.

Southern Baptists strongly emphasize both their Sunday school programs and the need for outreach through them. They are known and respected also for a number of different kinds of missionary work. Carter got involved in evangelism and church planning when he agreed to give a week with "no strings attached" and was sent north once a year by the Southern Baptist agency that coordinates such activity. When Carter talks about his commitment to Christ, he is likely to bring up the name of Eloy Cruz, a Cuban Christian with whom he ministered on one of the missions in the North. He quickly came to admire Cruz, and when it was time to part, Carter asked how such a tough and rugged man could be so loving. Through his embarrassment at the question, Cruz made the reply that Carter frequently passes on: "Senor Jaime, Nuestro Salvador tiene los manos que son muy suaves, y El no puede hacer mucho con un hombre que es dura." (Our Savior has hands which are very gentle, and he cannot do much with a man who is hard.)

Losing an election for governor in 1966 was a humbling experience for Carter. He admitted to times when he was overtaken by pride. He also conceded that since he was a small child he had been tempted to judge other people without charity—ever since he distinguished between good and bad people solely on the criterion of whether they bought a bag of boiled peanuts from him.

The loss was particularly tough for Carter because he had planned at first to run for Congress and probably would have been elected easily. The congressional seat had been held by Howard (Bo) Callaway, a natural rival of Carter's and the first Republican sent to Washington from that part of the country in more than a century. Callaway gave up the seat to run for governor and thus left Carter, who was by then building popularity of his own, with a clear shot to be chosen U.S. representative. But some friends urged him to challenge Callaway, arguing that only Carter could stop him and promising money. Carter finally agreed, but he notes that the financial support never came.

Callaway, also a native of southwest Georgia, graduated from West Point three years after Carter finished Annapolis. One major difference between them was that Callaway was born into wealth, heir to a textile fortune. Carter failed in the Democratic primary, losing to former Governor Ellis Arnall and segregationist restaurant-owner Lester Maddox. Carter was disheartened for a time but picked up the pieces and began long-range plans for an all-out gubernatorial effort in 1970.

Callaway received more votes than any other candidate in the general election but not a majority; so the state legislature named Maddox the winner. A sad sequel to the Carter-Callaway rivalry was that Callaway, named to head President Ford's campaign organization in 1976, was obliged to leave the post during the primaries because conflict-of-interest had been alleged in connection with Callaway's promotion of a Colorado ski resort he owned jointly with a brother-in-law. Carter had been among those who recommended Callaway for appointment as Secretary of the Army under President Nixon.

Carter said he and his wife shook hands with more than six hundred thousand people in Georgia—more than half the number of voters—in the 1970 gubernatorial race. His campaign was clearly in the context of trying to be a mediating and cooling influence in a troubled state, but many influential observers still expected the candidate to draw the old issue lines sharply. They were therefore troubled over the campaign rhetoric and strategy. Some tactics were subsequently "discovered" and then brought up again to haunt him as the 1976 primaries got under way.

Carter admits to having made mistakes. The worst, he says, was writing an ill-tempered letter to an Atlanta newspaper. Carter felt the editor had tried to characterize him as an ignorant, bigoted redneck. The newspaper did not print the letter, but Carter made it public by reading it to a meeting of the Georgia Press Association. That proved counterproductive, but Carter nevertheless won the election handily.

Carter's eight-minute inauguration speech was widely quoted and heralded as representative of the dawning of a new South. Said Carter:

"At the end of a long campaign, I believe I know the people of this state as well as anyone. Based on this knowledge of Georgians north and south, rural and urban, liberal and conservative, I say to you quite frankly that the time for racial discrimination is over. Our people have already made this major and difficult decision, but we cannot underestimate the challenge of hundreds of minor decisions yet to be made. Our inherent human charity and our religious beliefs will be taxed to the limit. No poor, rural, weak, or black person should ever have to bear the additional burden of being deprived of the opportunity of an education, a job, or simple justice."

As governor of Georgia, Carter spearheaded a reorganization of the executive branch of the state government and set out to improve the criminal justice system. Prison educational programs were multiplied fourfold. He established "zero-based budgeting," which meant that agencies had to justify all funding requests, not merely those for new or expanded programs.

Probably the most progress was achieved in the area of race relations. Carter worked to get better-educated people in positions of responsibility and found dozens of qualified black people to fill important posts. In a special gesture, he added portraits of notable blacks to the previously all-white galleries in the state office building.

Carter not only had Georgia on his mind but in his heart and soul. A *Christian Life* article quotes Carter's sister: "I remember asking him when he was still governor if he'd call a friend of mine and say hello the next time he was in New York. I later asked my friend if Jimmy had called. She said he'd called three times one day before he finally got her. They talked for 30 minutes. She told him about her son who had a drug problem and was living in Atlanta. When Jimmy got back home he called this woman's son and invited him out to the governor's mansion. He counselled the young man, and it straightened out his whole life."

As Billy Graham remarked when asked if Carter were "wearing his religion on his sleeve" during the campaign, "I don't believe it's on his sleeve, I believe it is in his heart." That was after Carter, in a political appearance in North Carolina, Graham's home state, made some remarks about his religious beliefs and experiences that were picked up by the news media and circulated literally around the world.

Carter and Graham have known each other but have not been close. In 1972, Carter told the United Methodist General Conference that Graham "has had a great impression and impact on my own life" and then went on to describe an experience in 1966 in connection with showing one of the evangelist's dramatic films: "I was asked to head up a mission program in my home county, the county seat of which is Americus. We had had a lot of racial problems in Americus and I was a little bit reluctant to do it. The effort was one with which you are familiar—the use of a movie film, *The Restless Ones.* I saw the film and really wasn't impressed by it. But we organized thoroughly in accordance with the standard procedures under Billy Graham's movement and we had that film for one week. It happened to have been the first interracial religious effort in the history of our county. We had 565 people who came forward to express their commitment to Christ: 137 of them accepted Christ for the first time. This encouraged me to realize that our own efforts cannot be controlled by a simple film which is really not of so much moment or my own faltering efforts, but that the Holy Spirit was there and people were changed."

Many evangelicals believe that social progress invariably results from truly effective evangelism. The model personality for a wedding of the two concerns has been William Wilberforce, a well-known British figure of the late eighteenth and early nineteenth centuries. Wilberforce was associated with the Clapham Sect, a group of evangelicals active in public life. He himself was aggressively evangelistic as well as being in the forefront of efforts aimed at social betterment. As a Member of Parliament he was credited with bringing an end to slave trade in 1807. Complete abolition of slavery came just before his death in 1833.

Donald W. Dayton explores comparable efforts on the American scene in *Discovering an Evangelical Heritage.* Dayton contends that nineteenth-century evangelicals were much more concerned about discharging their ethical responsibilities in national life than are those who regard themselves as evangelicals in the latter part of the twentieth century. He cites as ardent abolitionists the names of Jonathan Blanchard, first president of Wheaton College, and Charles G. Finney, one of the most famous evangelists in American history.

Evangelicals do have blind spots, some more apparent than others, and there was what an outsider might call social retrogression in the early part of this century when in the face of theological liberalism it became necessary to argue for more attention to doctrinal issues. The pivotal question has been: What does the Scripture teach? Southern Baptists as well as evangelicals as a whole have been referred to many, many times as "people of the Book." That does not mean that they subscribe to a paper pope, as some have put it, but they do try to keep in the foreground the premise that somewhere there must be a final appeal with reference to spiritual knowledge. For evangelicals, it is the Bible. Some modern issues are treated less than exhaustively in the Bible, and the result is that evangelicals differ in their interpretations. Good leadership is needed to avert fragmentation.

By staying close to Plains, figuratively as well as literally, Jimmy Carter demonstrates the urgency of not getting beyond where people are in their thinking. Generous amounts of patience are required, as are insights into the seriousness of divisive questions. The risk is that in trying to bring people along and bring them together into a greater enlightenment one may be called fuzzy or even unprincipled. Too much concentration on sheer principle, on the other hand, has the psychological effect of alienating those who disagree to the extent that they stubbornly refuse to assimilate information that might turn them around. What continues to challenge Carter is the problem of adhering to truth without letting it become a wedge.

3

Who Believes . . .

WITH NO group in the United States has the Carter phenomenon interacted more pronouncedly and more profoundly than with that part of the American religious spectrum which regards itself as evangelical.

With the arrival of spring only two days away, Carter stood on the patio of a sumptuous home in Winston-Salem, North Carolina, to give a little talk to a group of supporters. An amazingly large number of events favorable to him had come together to propel the Georgian into the lead in the race for the Democratic presidential nomination. Moreover, polls showed him preferred over Republican rivals by the whole electorate.

The next crucial juncture was the preference primary in North Carolina on March 23. The talk he was about to give would introduce a major new element into the 1976 political campaign —the religious issue. Reportedly, Carter's staff differed over whether to leave well enough alone. Part of the original strategy had been to run a steady, consistent campaign, building strength gradually and minimizing risks. Why should dealing with the religious aspect be considered a risk?

Winston-Salem, known primarily as a tobacco center but proud also of a rich religious heritage, was about to become something of a political landmark as well. Whatever the outcome, Carter was not playing it safe.

Carter told the group on the patio that evening that in 1967 he had undergone "a deeply profound religious experience that changed my life dramatically." In an account of the event by *Washington Post* staff writer Jules Witcover, Carter was quoted as saying, "I recognized for the first time that I had lacked something very precious—a complete commitment to Christ, a presence of the Holy Spirit in my life in a more profound and personal way. And since then I've had an inner peace and inner conviction and assurance that transformed my life for the better."

In an interview that night, Carter also told of a conversation with a younger sister in 1966 in which he expressed the desire for "inner peace." The sister, Mrs. Ruth Stapleton of Fayetteville, North Carolina, travels widely in a spiritual counseling ministry.

During a news conference the next day, in the capital city of Raleigh, Carter was asked to elaborate on his religious beliefs. According to Witcover, Carter said that in 1967 he felt his relationship with God "was very superficial . . . I came to realize that my Christian life, which I had always professed to be preeminent, had really been a secondary interest in my life. And I formed a very close, intimate personal relationship with God, through Christ, that has given me a great deal of peace, equanimity and the ability to accept difficulty without unnecessarily being disturbed, and also an inclination on a continuing basis to ask God's guidance in my life. It was not a profound stroke of miracle. It wasn't a voice of God from heaven. It was not anything of that kind. It wasn't mysterious. It might have been the same kind of experience as millions of people have who do become Christians in a deeply personal way."

Those millions cited by Carter are most readily classified as *evangelicals.* They can be distinguished primarily by the importance they attach to the Christian conversion experience.

Actually, Carter said nothing new in Winston-Salem. His personal devotion to Christianity and his participation in the affairs of his own denomination, the Southern Baptist Convention, were well understood by those at all familiar with Carter. Earlier that month *Time* had noted that he said he has been "twice born." The experiences referred to on the patio were recorded in detail in his autobiography, *Why Not the Best?*, which was beginning to get wide distribution. In December 1975 a *Newsweek* profile had quoted him as referring to himself as "a born-again Christian." As governor of Georgia, four years previously he had told the General Conference, the international legislative assembly of the United Methodist Church, that the single most important factor in his life was Jesus Christ.

What made the remarks so significant in Winston-Salem in mid-March was that they were coming from the front-runner for the Democratic presidential nomination, and no presidential candidate except William Jennings Bryan has been known to talk like that. In his study of campaign biographies, William Burlie Brown notes that the candidates in American presidential elections invariably come out religiously vague. Brown comments, "Yet the impression emerges that this vagueness does not emanate from any design to deceive. It is, rather, that sincere vagueness that appears to be endemic to religion in America—a nation that has spawned the most sects and the fewest theologians."

The town of Salem was founded in 1766 by devout Moravians who were not at all vague about what *they* believed. They were part of a zealous missionary movement begun earlier in the eighteenth century by Count Nikolaus von Zinzendorf, an Austrian nobleman, which traced its spiritual ancestry to the fifteenth-century Bohemian reformer John Huss. Salem remained under Moravian control until 1849. After it was merged with Winston in 1913, the Moravian community became a tiny ecclesiastical enclave in a burgeoning center of commerce dominated by Baptists and Methodists.

Moravians came on to the European and American scenes as the Puritans, America's original settlers, were losing vitality. The Moravians themselves went into decline as secular culture made God-talk increasingly indecorous. By the twentieth century, Western society expected intelligent and influential people to speak up on transitory issues but considered that specific convictions on eternal verities be kept private. They were regarded as of little or no earthly significance.

Concern over the beliefs of John F. Kennedy, the first Roman Catholic president in American history, coupled with considerable public discussion of the actions of Vatican Council II, brought religion in the lives of the people of the United States somewhat out in the open again. Yet Kennedy said little about his faith as such. He simply assured the American people that he supported the principle of separation of church and state, and he vowed not to impose Catholic principles upon the citizenry.

During the twentieth century evangelicals have been more than holding their own although they have been ignored for the most part by other religious groups and by society as a whole.

The term *evangelical* has long been used by theological conservatives within the Protestant tradition to describe themselves. It was not frequently applied to them by others until the 1960s when nonevangelicals seeking to open ecumenical dialogue began picking up the term, usually prefacing it with the adjective *conservative.* Religion reporters have given wide recognition.

Evangelicals are the spiritual descendants of the fundamentalists whose popularity or lack thereof reached a peak during the famous Scopes trial in 1925. Most American evangelicals in 1976 would say they share the basic doctrine of the fundamentalists but reject the narrow cultural outlook and obscurantism connected with them. The issue of evolution was not taken as seriously after 1925, and evangelicals in 1976, although continuing to insist on the integrity of the first chapters of Genesis, are more tolerant of one another's interpretations of the creation account.

In a widely quoted editorial that appeared in 1967, *Christianity Today* magazine estimated that about forty million Americans could be classified as or would classify themselves as evangelicals. Many informed evangelicals regard that estimate as too high, and a very few think it too low.

Evangelicals are found in many denominations and at virtually every economic and social level. They differ on a number of theological tenets, but there is at least one they affirm unanimously: Evangelicals believe that people are born in sin and are bound for a literal hell unless by faith they appropriate God's offer of salvation made possible by Christ's death and resurrection. This acceptance is normally regarded as an act of the will but is often accompanied by a prayer of confession and repentance. What happens may be called *redemption, conversion, commitment, decision for Christ,* or simply *belief.* The common theological term is *regeneration.*

Essentially, this particular doctrine is nothing more or less than classical, orthodox Christianity. Some churches not in the evangelical tradition attach assorted means and conditions to regeneration, or associate it with a process in life, or tend to neglect it. Universalist doctrine regards salvation as automatic for every human being.

Carter has won wide recognition as an evangelical without making any extensive statement that reproduces accurately what evangelicals would regard as an absolutely authentic testimony of regeneration. But he has come close enough, certainly closer than any American president has, in public, to satisfy many evangelicals that he is one of them.

Carter has impressed evangelicals, not only by talking about his own spiritual experiences, but by engaging in extensive Christian witnessing. Evangelicals put priority on evangelism, that is, on persuading people of the necessity for a personal, saving relationship to Christ. Evangelicals feel that human beings need more than anything else in this world to know that their sins are forgiven. Evangelicals are convinced that unless this is accomplished ultimate favor will not be bestowed. Evangelism takes place in mass crusade rallies, in church meetings, on radio and television, through literature distribution, and in person-to-person conversation. It is a matter of heaven to be gained and hell to be shunned.

When Carter speaks plainly about leading others to commitment, the words ring true. If it means taking a political chance, so be it.

As an adjective the term *evangelical* pertains to the gospel and goes back to the Greek term *euaggélion* which meant "good news" and was set apart for this unique usage by the divinely inspired writers of the New Testament. The noun *evangelical* therefore refers to one who is devoted to this good news. The content of this good news is believed to be associated with the provision for regeneration as summarized in 1 Corinthians 15:-1–4, the central message being that Christ died for our sins, was buried, then actually came back to life as prophesied in the Old Testament. And, as Handel's *Messiah* so movingly declares, "Because he lives, I too can live." Hence the evangelical emphasis on spiritual rebirth.

The words *evangelism, evangelist,* and *evangelical* are derived from the same root but in usage have become distinct, properly speaking. Whereas at one time to be evangelistic meant to proclaim the gospel, today one can be termed evangelistic by showing zeal for other things as well. Witnessing, preaching, or proclaiming (the words are virtually interchangeable) the gospel means attempting to persuade nonbelievers to understand their need of the Savior. A person is "won to Christ" and forgiven of sins when he or she exercises faith in the truth of the gospel and its power to save him or her.

Many Americans, even some churchgoers, seem to feel threatened when they hear this kind of message. Perhaps this stems partly from the fact that it was never put to them quite that way before. The good news is really news to them. "Preaching" laymen like Carter are particularly suspect because the average person tends to think of preaching as the exclusive prerogative of ordained clergy. Evangelicals hold, however, that witnessing is everybody's business. If spiritual salvation is as incomparably important as the Bible indicates, is it not the duty of everyone who knows it to pass on the word? Evangelicals feel their theology is the closest to that which first-century churches taught and that it has been essentially preserved to the present, though popular in some ages and unpopular in others. Contrary to prevalent opinion, most evangelicals make no special effort to add members to churches; placing names on rolls is secondary to evangelism.

Naturally, all this hinges on whether one believes the Bible to be a special revelation of God, and where this premise is disputed, there is bound to be an absence of evangelical teaching. Baptists, generally speaking, have been more faithful to orthodoxy than other Protestants, but by and large the old-line denominations are under the influence of a nonevangelical outlook. Many accommodate both evangelicals and nonevangelicals in their ranks. Theology, once regarded as the queen of the sciences, has become so diverse that it is difficult to single out a dominating view among leading scholars. Meanwhile, many churchgoers live and die without ever being meaningfully confronted with their personal need of the Savior.

Inasmuch as individual regeneration has been the one doctrine holding evangelicals together, it follows that this focus will be paramount when evangelicals get together. The World Congress on Evangelism in Berlin in 1966 and the 1974 International Congress on World Evangelization were key evangelical strategy sessions.

Anxiety sometimes arises over evangelism as it did over Carter. Some people feel they are being imposed upon. Such complaints were voiced in connection with Key 73, a cooperative evangelism outreach in which representatives from most major denominations in the United States and Canada had some involvement. Negative responses have also come up when numerous parachurch evangelistic organizations intensify efforts to recruit laymen all over the country.

Carter's reply to the anxiety is to stress that as a Baptist he believes in the separation of church and state and in the autonomy of the local congregation. In other words, he is prevented by the Constitution from making public policy out of ecclesiastical preference, and he is not bound by any decision of an ecclesiastical superior. Historically, Baptists have championed religious freedom. Not all evangelicals, to be sure, think like Carter on these issues; so the inquiry gets a bit complicated.

Actually, evangelicals do claim exclusivity with respect to the means of salvation, and they will resist any attempt to get them to back off that tenet. The one-way Jesus bumper stickers and decals reflect evangelical belief accurately because Scripture is understood as teaching it: "Neither is there salvation in any other: for there is none other name under heaven given among men, whereby we must be saved" (Acts 4:12).

This is *not* something to be feared by nonevangelicals, for authentic Christian evangelism proceeds on a purely voluntary premise. Indeed, Christians often tell one another that their job is not to get people converted but to offer them the gospel in a way that they can understand it best. Much strain over controversial doctrines has been occasioned by the theological illiteracy of the twentieth century brought on by the notion that religious views should not be discussed openly outside churches, synagogues, or private homes. In a very real sense every person claims an exclusivity; even to say that beliefs are not important is a point of view in itself which presupposes that it is error to say otherwise.

Thinking Christians wonder what specific actions could be feared from an evangelical president. With Judaism, the evangelical ethos affirms the Ten Commandments. It is hard to imagine what program an evangelical in power might impose that a Jew would find religiously oppressive or offensive or that would be out of harmony with the classic Judeo-Christian outlook. Curtailments which Puritans felt necessary to impose upon dissenters at the outset of the American experience were largely dissolved, just as Jewish authorities gradually eased restrictions upon non-Jews after the early days of the modern state of Israel.

Christians do not believe, as is sometimes alleged, that fellow believers *necessarily* make the best officeholders. For one thing, since there is no sure way to tell who is a Christian (only God really knows) and who is not, there is no magic in urging votes for Christians. "The tension is relieved even further," said a lead editorial in *Christianity Today,* "by the realization that some non-Christians behave more in keeping with the Bible than do some Christians. . . . Christians should not automatically vote for Christians because they are Christians any more than Jews should vote in a bloc for Jews. God works through unconverted as well as coverted persons to execute his perfect will; his purpose is not thwarted nor his sovereignty diminished by human rejection of or indifference to the Gospel."

A help to understanding this is to keep in mind that in the evangelical view salvation is by God's grace and not through works, that is, good deeds. Evangelicals contend that their central message of making peace with God provides a person with what is sometimes described as the "power source" for ethical conduct. It might also be referred to as the enabling for proper conduct, and if nonevangelicals feel they have an adequate alternative for this enabling, then mutual respect is certainly possible.

Neither Carter nor any other responsible evangelical candidate feels that his or her religious faith provides infallible solutions to complex twentieth-century problems. A number of various avenues lead toward answers to the contemporary human and social dilemma. One would hope that Carter's commitment to Christ will give him at the very least a profound sense of justice and a determination to be consistent. One wonders whether what the nation needs is to persevere on one course, even if that proves to be a longer road. Carter often cites the political inclination to "halt between two opinions" so that no prospect is ever followed through thoroughly enough to see if it would work. Martin Marty, the always-arresting Lutheran scholar who is associate editor of the *Christian Century,* concluded: "When 30 economists are polled and they all say something different, the only thing the public can be sure of is that nobody really knows the answers to our problems. So they figure maybe it will help if they just get a decent, religious man in office."

The state has been the one human institution in a place to inhibit or guarantee religious rights. One might say that the task was to define those rights or to establish the boundaries of the religious realm upon which civil authority must not encroach. Some Christians, however, have felt that it might be fruitful to reverse the approach and ask, Where is Caesar's place in the religious realm?

Whatever one's religion, its authority extends beyond and above the state (unless one's religion *is* the state). If it does not, then it is not really religion because one's religion is that set of beliefs one considers supremely important.

Regrettably, church history abounds with cases in which Christians took unfair advantage of people with whom they had religious differences. Carter is finding that Christians are going to be a long time living those down Past indiscretions of believers have not helped his campaign.

Does evangelistic proclamation per se trample upon the religious rights of non-Christians? If Christians are unable to say no clearly, then a prolonged and bitter dispute is inevitable. What's more, Christians then have no basis for seeking government protection against ideological assaults from others and no ground on which to claim a freedom to preach the gospel in other cultures. A pluralistic society has a right to know exactly where Christians stand.

Christian coercion and Christian conversion are antithetical. Where there is coercion, there is no genuine conversion. The Christian call requires freedom of choice. It must always be put as Joshua stated it: "*Choose* you this day whom ye will serve" (Josh. 24:15, italics mine). Orthodox, reformed Christianity never recognizes as true believers those who identified with the church out of misunderstanding, ulterior motives, or coercion. For a Christian therefore to try to force his or her will upon another regarding conversion is pointless.

Communist theoreticians pose an intellectually suicidal response to the challenge of religious freedom. They have belittled religious belief, maintaining that it exists only as a temporary relief from oppressive social conditions and will disappear when economic justice is achieved. But every person places some aspect of reality above all others. Paul Tillich's description of religion as "ultimate concern" was a convenient modern term for an entity long recognized. The U.S. Supreme Court approvingly quoted Tillich's view that religion is "what you take seriously without any reservation." Medieval philosophers spoke of "that than which no greater can be thought" and thus described God. Christians in Communist lands have a powerful, rational argument in seeking greater freedom for religious expression. Evangelicals believe that people may differ on the object of their greatest allegiance, but every human being does give such an allegiance. What you doubt the least is what you worship.

Absolute freedom is impossible and undesirable. Simply to preserve meaning, all human activities must be restrained within some bounds of purpose and propriety. It is no more reasonable to say that a person ought to be able to do anything than it is to say that a train should not have to run on tracks. The one recorded instance of applied anarchism (see Judg. 17:6) is reliably reported to have ended in failure.

Carter has done a great service to the country by attracting attention to the question of religious liberty because it is the most basic of human freedoms and to withhold it is to exercise the worst kind of repression possible. Yet virtually everyone would agree that there must be boundaries. Where do we draw the line? Should one have the freedom to blow up buildings on the grounds that it is somehow a religious exercise?

The crux of the matter lies in social significance. Human beings are generally inclined in this day and age to grant freedom of belief if its expression has no discernible effects upon others. If there are social consequences, then the state is invariably called upon to regulate the outward expressions of the belief. In the interests of order and of checking evil, the church must yield to civil authority.

This seems like putting the state over the church, a binding of God's principles, and there has been intense debate on the subject ever since Constantine recognized Christianity as the religion of the Roman Empire in A.D. 311. Carter has recognized these still very gray areas and has not claimed any special expertise to deal with them. The Christian's consolation is that government in general has been explicitly ordained of God. Most Bible exegetes agree on that.

Beyond such consideration, it is hard to talk in terms of legal absolutes. Obviously, codes indispensable to Manhattan Island (population: 1,500,000) may be quite irrelevant on Pitcairn Island (population: 85). Much rests with the degree of responsibility assumed by the citizenry. The numbers and kinds of laws in operation must be the product of a democratically arrived-at consensus.

Everyone thinks his or her way is the best way, and whether evangelical or otherwise, everyone deserves the chance to tell why. The Christian simply gets in line with everyone else trying to be convincing that his or her choice is desirable for everyone. The Western world has an adequate system of law to handle this input.

Evangelicals propagate their ethic under an implicit reciprocity agreement. This has troubled some Christians because it may seem to imply that evil has rights, but here the question comes back to the principle of voluntarism, which has biblical support in the Golden Rule. Allowing equal opportunity for competing principles is not inconsistent with Christian principles. Rather, it fulfills one of those principles, namely, that people should be allowed to choose for themselves.

The fallacy to be avoided is the notion that principles of sectarian origin have no right of recognition in law. This idea flies in the face of our whole past because much present law in the democratic countries of the world is rooted in Judeo-Christian teaching. When was the cutoff date for religious influence? People who suggest that "religious dogma must not be injected into national policy or political strategy" must be urged to think a little harder because *everyone* has a set of religious beliefs (they may be materialistic or spiritual) as a base from which to act, whether he or she realizes it or not. Would it not be smarter to recognize that our choice is not religion or no religion, but which religion?

Understandably, Carter has avoided this philosophical thicket, but evangelicals are obliged to raise the questions because it is they who have been called obscurantist and irrational in the past. Now it appears that so-called religionless thought is what is contrary to logic. The real culprit is not that antireligionists consciously seek to be antiintellectual but that for years they have avoided any serious study of religion and are therefore proceeding on premises long ago ruled meaningless.

Robert Brow argues that to be religious requires only faith in some kind of meaning. His book *Religion* shows the essence of some supposedly modern outlooks to be twenty-five hundred years old. He adds, "Even if a scientist's only article of faith is 'I believe in progress,' he is still religious. He has a faith, a goal, a system of ethics and a religious experience which take him up into something greater than his own nothingness."

Assuming that the American outlook presupposes the affirmation of meaning and is therefore religious in some sense, evangelicals find disconcerting the common current political practice of disqualifying ideas deemed sectarian in origin. How can the nation perpetuate any rationale for values with such an attitude? Should not ideas be judged on their merit?

Three months before declaring his presidential candidacy, Carter as governor of Georgia attended a reenactment of the 1774 First Continental Congress in Carpenter's Hall, Philadelphia. The governors of all thirteen original states were there listening to the same prayer and sitting in the same chairs as did those first leaders of what was to become the United States. Carter has since related the experience a number of times, saying that he had thought soberly about those early days and compared them to the nation two hundred years later. He said he wondered to himself, among other things, "Did they have deeper religious convictions?"

"I think not," Carter said in an address to the National Press Club. "We are equally capable of correcting our faults, overcoming difficulties, managing our own affairs and facing the future with justifiable confidence. I am convinced that among us 200 million Americans there is a willingness—even eagerness—to restore in our country what has been lost—if we have understandable purposes and goals and a modicum of bold and inspired leadership."

If there is a religious dimension to the desired recovery, as Carter implied, then a better understanding is in order, not only of the beliefs of the founding fathers of the 1770s, but of the settlers and explorers before them. The First Amendment ruled out establishment of religion, but throughout its history the American government has encouraged the churches (through such means as tax exemption) to contribute their influence to the national dynamic. One of the main reasons is the underpinning of the evangelical ethos dating back to the nation's earliest history.

When the first Europeans sloshed ashore in the New World, they brought along evangelistic fervor and missionary zeal. We have often lost sight of this spiritual aspect of the initial explorations. Thanks to the emphases of the American public school system, we have learned more instead of the effort by Columbus and his party to find an ocean route to the wealth of the East.

"But even the most practical promoters [of the venture] looked for something more," wrote the distinguished historian Samuel Eliot Morison. "They hoped to convert the heathen to Christianity."

As evangelicals in the bicentennial year made themselves more aware of this background, they understood better that their relative well-being in the world was a special favor from God. Certainly one cannot dispute that both the United States and Canada have prospered materially and otherwise. Where else in the world do conditions equal those in North America? Because of our good fortune we are tempted toward pride, but we have also become blasé, and we groan inwardly when bombarded with constant reminders of our national heritage and the concomitant good life. Americans with naturalized citizenship or with foreign-born parents feel more keenly about these things because they have had more exposure to how the other half lives.

In recent years, much discussion of America's religious orientation centered on the Declaration of Independence, the Constitution, and the faith of Washington, Franklin, Jefferson, and Madison. There was much more, however, to the American ethos. The moral nature of the nation could not be adequately reflected in a pair of relatively brief political documents, no matter how well drawn, nor could it be deduced from the beliefs of the few men who shaped these documents.

An evangelical ethos was spread through a broad spectrum of colonial culture, having built momentum for the better part of three centuries before the Declaration of Independence was proclaimed. One of the major marks engraved upon that ethos was the deeply held conviction that efforts must be exerted to proclaim the gospel.

Christopher Columbus, whose very name means "Christ bearer," called the island where he landed San Salvador (Holy Savior), and the appellation stuck. His standing as one literally bearing Christ and therefore an evangelist was apparent in his description of overtures made to the Indians there: "In order that we might win good friendship, because I knew that they were a people who could better be freed and converted to our Holy Faith by love than by force, I gave to some of them red caps and to some glass beads, which they hung on their necks, and many other things of slight value, in which they took much pleasure."

The following year Columbus wrote to Spain's general treasurer: "Let Christ rejoice on earth as He rejoices in heaven in the prospect of the salvation of the souls of so many nations hitherto lost." Unfortunately, subsequent treatment of Indians in the New World was disgraceful, and Christians became indifferent to their plight.

A patent granted by Emperor Charles V to a would-be settler in Florida in the early part of the sixteenth century perpetuated the spiritual concern: "Whereas our principal intent in the discovery of new lands is that the inhabitants and natives thereof, who are without the light or knowledge of faith, may be brought to understand the truths of our holy Catholic faith, that they may come to a knowledge thereof and become Christians and be saved, and this is the chief motive that you are to bear and hold in this affair . . ." Clifton E. Olmstead, in his *History of Religion in the United States,* wrote that despite encountering "almost insuperable difficulties" in the settlement at St. Augustine the work grew. By 1634, there were twenty-five thousand native converts. Such success was extraordinary, most missionaries to Indians saying that resistance was great (which did not affect evangelistic intensity). One researcher has called the Navajos "the most missionaried people in the world."

While those early explorers were negotiating the Atlantic for the sake of both the gospel and the gold, the Reformation, and subsequently the Counter-Reformation, was taking place in Europe. Thousands of people were drawn to the Bible. Theoretically, at least, evangelism took priority in the hearts of the devout. In actual everyday life, however, the urgency of Christian outreach often took second place in practical terms, especially among church leaders, because of the intensity of the theological warfare between Protestants and Catholics. Luther and Calvin, for example, were not particularly noted for capitalizing upon opportunities to implement what down through the centuries came to be known as the Great Commission. This evangelistic imperative was issued by Christ to his disciples: "Go, then, to all peoples everywhere and make them my disciples: baptize them in the name of the Father, the Son, and the Holy Spirit, and teach them to obey everything I have commanded you. And remember! I will be with you always, to the end of the age" (Matt. 28:19–20, *Today's English Version*).

No Protestant denomination has supported as many overseas missionaries as the Southern Baptist Convention of which Carter is a part, and he himself made trips which he recalls as resulting in the deepening of his own spiritual being as well as fulfilling the Great Commission.

Such activity was much more commonplace and common knowledge when a foothold was being established in the New World. The contemporary evangelical writer James C. Hefley, in an otherwise first-rate book, *America: One Nation under God,* minimizes the spiritual factor in the first English settlement at Jamestown, contending that "the Virginians came mainly to exploit the natural wealth of the New World." There is good historical evidence to dispute such a conclusion.

Three ships landed at Jamestown, one of which was named *Godspeed.* An aim of the supporting company is given by no less an authority than *Encyclopedia Britannica* as being "to spread the Gospel among the heathen people of Virginia." Robert Hunt, an Anglican clergyman, was among those who disembarked. He conducted the initial Communion service on May 14, 1607. A church was among the first buildings erected, and a reproduction incorporating part of the ruins can be viewed today. As early as 1610, Virginia colonists were connecting missionary work with conquest and barter, which seems out of place for twentieth-century people but which was quite natural during times when religion was not as compartmentalized.

Evangelicals believe that God honors those who spread his Word and that he also blesses those who do not take credit for themselves but offer him thanks for whatever prosperity is experienced. As Carter has said, "We, as Americans, in this tough, competitive world, have learned to be aggressive, manly, and unafraid. Because of this, we have developed a pride in our own toughness and thus our priorities have sometimes become distorted." Associating religion with searching, Carter quotes Tillich, adding, "The thing I get out of it is, at the time that we quit searching and think we know the answers, when we think we are self-reliant, perhaps at that moment we lose part of our religion." The latter comment, articulated at the United Methodist General Conference, echoed a caution of the sort that occasioned Thanksgiving commemorations at Jamestown and Plymouth and eventually evolved into yearly observances. Canadians also celebrate a Thanksgiving Day.

Religious strife in Europe, as is well known, prompted the sailing of the Mayflower. Here was a shipload of separatists intent on establishing a community in the New World in which they could worship as they pleased. Before landing, the group covenanted together in a "civil body politic" which subsequently came to be called the Mayflower Compact, one of the truly remarkable historical documents of all time. It notes, significantly, that the voyage had been undertaken "for the glory of God and advancement of the Christian faith" as well as for the honor of king and country.

Much data could be adduced to show the evangelistic drive of the settlers, particularly among Indians. What is generally considered the most memorable work among Indians was done by John Eliot, who dedicated his life to the cause in 1646 and saw some four thousand conversions in thirty years. The converts were gathered into twenty-four congregations, some with ordained Indian ministers. The first Bible printed in America in any language was the one Eliot produced in a translation for the Massachusetts Algonkian Indians. There has been a strong outreach tradition among evangelical American Indians ever since, and in 1975 they held an interdenominational leadership and evangelism conference at which time they inaugurated a continuing organization.

The colonizers organized themselves with similar goals. A royal charter was granted in 1701 for the "Society for the Propagation of the Gospel in Foreign Parts," the objective of which was to minister mainly to the colonies, evangelizing both Indians and slaves.

Schools in the colonies were founded around the same purpose. Even the great universities, which subsequently were secularized, had evangelistic roots. Harvard College, founded in 1636 to train ministers of the gospel, adopted as one of the rules and precepts for students: "Everyone shall consider the main end of his life and studies to know God and Jesus Christ, which is eternal life."

In 1693 England's sovereigns, William and Mary, granted a charter to the college in Virginia which bears their name, stating that "our well-beloved and faithful subjects, constituting the General Assembly of our colony of Virginia, have had it in their minds, and have proposed to themselves, to the end that the Church of Virginia may be furnished with a seminary of ministers of the Gospel, and that the youth may be piously educated in good letters and manners, and that the Christian faith may be propagated amongst the Western Indians, to the glory of Almighty God."

Yale was constituted in 1701 in recognition of the fact that the colonies had been established "both to plant and under the Divine Blessing to propagate in this wilderness, the blessed reformed Protestant religion, in the purity of its order and worship, not only to their prosperity, but also to the barbarous natives."

The Great Awakening, a revival in the colonies that crested in 1740, has been called "the inner American revolution, a spiritual declaration of independence that made the political reshuffling thirty-six years later an inevitability." So said Mark Noll in an article in *Christianity Today.* One wonders if it was not a declaration of *de*pendence upon God on the part of much of the citizenry that brought the colonies through all their difficulties. Whatever else may be said about the Puritans, they certainly had a degree of discipline rivaled by few people in recorded human history, and only discipline could have overcome the rigors they faced.

The vices of the colonial days have been well documented, and there is no point in pretending that the forefathers were sinlessly perfect. What is significant is that an influential segment recognized the fallenness of man and, therefore, their evangelistic responsibility. The resurgence of the evangelical ethos promises creative implementation in America's third century with a special focus upon biblical ethics. Only to the extent that such ties are established is there hope for impact upon the culture approximating that of early American thinkers such as Jonathan Edwards.

Edwards is popularly remembered for a hellfire sermon hardly characteristic of him and certainly not doing him justice as one of the great minds in American history. Recent scholarship has helped to bring about a more worthy perspective. Yale professor Perry Miller's biography of Edwards, a modern classic, notes that Edwards was a philosopher and a theologian and infinitely more. "He was one of America's five or six major artists," said Miller, "who happened to work with ideas instead of with poems or novels." Edwards treated topics "in the manner of the very finest speculators, in the manner of Augustine, Aquinas, and Pascal, as problems not of dogma but of life."

Historian Morison, citing the especially remarkable facets of Edwards, calls his account of conversion at the age of seventeen "one of the most beautiful records of that Christian phenomenon since St. Augustine." Edwards might have been a naturalist or a great literary figure, Morison adds, "but he chose theology because he believed that an exploration of the relation between man and God was infinitely more important. He would have considered our modern efforts to explore outer space as of minor importance, since their objects are merely to extend human knowledge. He looked beyond all stellar systems and galaxies, to save men's souls for eternal life."

Edwards not only talked about evangelism but engaged in it. Following the Great Awakening he and his wife and eight children moved to the frontier settlement of Stockbridge in the Berkshire Hills to minister to a small Indian reservation. As E. Brooks Holifield has put it, "New England Puritans required of one another a set of inward religious experiences; admission to their churches depended on a credible narration of 'conversion,' which they defined as 'regeneration' or 'rebirth.' " Holifield, Emory University, made the statements in his *New Republic* article tracing the strands of Carter's religion. Holifield asserted that "the Southern Baptist Convention is among the last great repositories of the Puritan tradition in America." Denominationally speaking, that is true, but the repository is more accurately cast in the community which regards itself as evangelical and embraces Southern Baptists as well as others.

The point is that Edwards wedded mind and spirit, the ideal that many thinking evangelicals are championing more than two hundred years later. Edwards worked under the influence of John Locke, who stressed experience and the appeal to empirical data over the emphasis on reason taught by the early modern philosophers such as Descartes and Spinoza. The American outlook is really a marriage of these foci, and Edwards may yet be discovered as having a good deal to do with shaping and arranging the match. Most analysts agree that Edwards would have come up with an awesome, powerful systematic had he lived longer.

The influence of Edwards notwithstanding, other influences were also at work in America's development. Some say there were two sets of founding fathers. Undoubtedly deists as well as evangelicals presided at the nation's birth. But the fact remains that an evangelical ethos has been at work in a major way in the history of the land. Evangelicals have a rich heritage. In the year 1976 that heritage begins to look as if it will blossom once again.

Carter has spoken with a number of evangelical groups, readily identifying his faith with theirs. The international General Council of the Christian and Missionary Alliance met in Atlanta in 1974 while Carter was still governor of Georgia. The CMA is a small denomination but supports nearly one thousand missionaries overseas. In an address to this group, Carter said, "My family, my business customers, the people of Georgia know that the most important thing in my life is Jesus Christ. And I know that you share my firm conviction as those who have a strong missionary spirit, that the most important pursuit for us in this present life and for eternity is to let others know about the grace of God in our own lives and what it can mean to them."

Nathan Bailey, CMA president, responded in a way that presaged evangelical enthusiasm about Carter on a national scale: "Governor Carter, on behalf of the delegates and visitors . . . I wish to thank you most sincerely. . . . It has been so obviously and evidently an expression of a warm-hearted, dedicated Christian man in public life. I'm sure none of us want to mix politics with this occasion, but regardless of our party affiliation, Governor, I hope if the Lord tarries, that all of us will have opportunity to vote for you for some national office sometime in the future."

As a presidential candidate, Carter has been careful not to exploit the evangelical context, even though many doors would have readily opened for him. George McGovern spoke in 1972 at Wheaton College, the best-known and most respected evangelical institution of higher learning, and President Ford delivered an address there in 1976. During the primary campaign Carter attended Sunday church services regularly, in Plains and elsewhere, but did not appear to go out of his way to arrange publicized religious meetings. The 1976 session of Carter's own Southern Baptist Convention was host for a Ford speech (Carter did appear at an SBC session in Dallas in 1973). As a whole, Carter has spoken about religion only in response to questions.

When asked if as president he would seek and depend on God's guidance, Carter gave an unequivocal yes. He said that as he gained more responsibility during his life he spent more time "on my knees in prayer."

National Courier correspondent Quin Sherrer quoted Carter as saying, "I'm a born-again Christian and I don't want anything that's not God's will for my life."

Carter went on to say that he thought the evangelical Christians of America "even if they don't know me or belong to a different party are to some degree at least searching for a reinstitution of what has been lost in this country."

The next question posed to him was, "Why have we gone so far from our founding fathers' principles of Christianity?"

Carter's answer, as relayed by Sherrer, was: "It's two-fold. Some of our leaders have betrayed the trust of the people who elected them. Secondly, there has been a general absence of a continuing commitment to those high principles. I think Americans have to be reminded continuously of what our nation is with its shortcomings and what it ought to be—always better."

Carter reaffirmed to Sherrer that if he ever found any conflict between his faith and politics he would give up politics, but Carter added, "I think everyone of us in our own lives has inherent conflicts built in as we equate our Christian beliefs with our worldly responsibilities. I've found when I reassert my relationship with God, conflicts disappear."

When interviewed by Jim Newton, editor of *World Mission Journal,* Carter declared, "I believe God wants me to be the best politician I can possibly be."

Did Carter think he would win the presidency because God was on his side? "Well, I do think I will win, but I've never asked God to let me win. I've always prayed that I will be able to do the right thing whether I win or lose. I do pray frequently during the day."

Carter has always tried to answer even the toughest questions in easy terms and plain language. To talk of his faith seems to come naturally. When he does, it is widely reported, and evangelicals are gratified. Those who are not reticent or self-conscious like to talk that way themselves because the relationship they feel with their Creator and Redeemer is the most important aspect of their lives. Some traditional evangelical churches and some churches who have welcomed the Jesus people in recent years have "testimony meetings" in their regular services. They share spiritual thoughts and feelings, giving thanks to God for past occurrences and asking prayer support for upcoming opportunities and problems.

Personal piety figures prominently in the life of the average evangelical. He or she senses the need to read and study the Bible each day and to set aside times for prayer. The evangelical is often noticeable in restaurants when he or she bows for a brief prayer of gratitude before meals. Wednesday night prayer meetings are still going strong in virtually all evangelical churches, including Carter's congregation in Plains.

Evangelicals avoid profanity, and most feel strongly about it. Indeed, the revelation in the Watergate tapes that President Nixon made such generous use of obscene language was unquestionably a major reason for the loss of confidence in him by the evangelical community. That kind of talk did not jibe with the image put forth by worship services in the White House.

There are a number of other evangelical taboos of varying intensity according to time and place. These have been placed in a most constructive context in a standards-of-conduct document recently adopted by Wheaton College as reflective of the evangelical consensus. Certain behavior such as stealing and dishonesty, along with attitudes such as greed and prejudice, are seen as explicity prohibited by Scripture. Other forbidden practices are seen not as specifically barred by the Bible but as harmful or offensive to others (for example, drinking and gambling). A third category touches upon movie attendance and viewing, dancing, and card playing; discretion and restraint are to be exercised in participating in these activities. Proper use of Sunday also is included in the latter category.

Jimmy Carter is seen as a man at least respectful and supportive of such a life-style although he does not condemn others in these respects. He tries to assign proper priorities and to concentrate on what counts the most.

Carter, though not a tall man, takes long strides literally and figuratively. One of his strides in the primary campaign was a victory in North Carolina. Just ahead in the following month were key contests in large Northern states. These would indicate not only how many steps he still had to take to capture his party's nomination but would also suggest how much voter appeal he could muster in the general election. How would he do in labor-oriented ethnic concentrations outside the Bible Belt, in industrial areas where the evangelical ethos had less recognition? A column by Joseph Kraft appearing in the *Washington Post* on the day of the Winston-Salem event reminded Carter that his qualities were about to be tested "in areas where Baptist rhetoric runs way behind bread and ideology."

4

That It Is Time . . .

THE MOST important factors behind Carter's rise include a number of fascinating developments on the American scene. In themselves these events were quite outside the scope of his immediate influence, but in some cases he sensed their significance more acutely than did the other candidates and therefore capitalized upon them.

The most intensive phase of Carter's primary campaign began in January 1976. He had been traveling and speaking strenuously for about a year, but now he had to induce an even greater flow of adrenalin for the 2,350 precinct caucuses in Iowa that month and the traditional first state primary in New Hampshire in February.

"I visited 110 towns in Iowa and my wife went to 150," Carter often said thereafter.

Meanwhile, a seemingly unrelated drama was unfolding which would indirectly but nevertheless quite remarkably enhance Carter's appeal.

Charles Colson, President Nixon's noted hatchet man, stood at a tenth-floor window overlooking the White House. He was visiting the editorial offices of *Christianity Today* located just a block from his former place of employment. It was the dead of winter, and with no leaves on the trees to block the line of vision, the resplendent executive mansion revered the world over was in full view. Only a year before Colson had been released from seven months of imprisonment for obstructing justice. He had come that afternoon to meet with a group of editors and describe the spiritual transformation that had taken place in his life to transcend the ignominy of Watergate.

"Born again" was the best way to put it. Indeed, Colson used the term as the title of the 351-page book that he wrote to explain how he got into the mess and how he turned to God to pull him out of it.

Colson was counseled about his need of a personal relationship with Christ by an old friend, Tom Phillips, president of Raytheon Corporation. Phillips gave Colson a book to read, *Mere Christianity* by C. S. Lewis. Phillips himself had been converted at a Billy Graham rally in Madison Square Garden several years before. Colson took the book and read it while vacationing on the coast of Maine, half expecting it to represent an intuitive, emotional approach to God. Instead he found the author's intellect "so disciplined, so lucid, so relentlessly logical that I could only be grateful I had never faced him in a court of law."

Colson invited Christ into his mind and heart early one Friday morning while he sat alone staring out at the ocean. He recalls the words: "Lord Jesus, I believe You. I accept You. Please come into my life. I commit it to You."

In *Born Again,* Colson records that "With these few words that morning, while the briny sea churned, came a sureness of mind that matched the depth of feeling in my heart. There came something more: strength and serenity, a wonderful new assurance about life, a fresh perception of myself and the world around me. In the process, I felt old fears, tensions, and animosities draining away. I was coming alive to things I'd never seen before; as if God was filling the barren void I'd known for so many months, filling it to its brim with a whole new kind of awareness."

Born Again became an instant best seller in the religious trade and soon pushed its way onto the shelves of secular bookstores as well. It seemed that in the aftermath of Watergate a spiritual quest had developed on a national scale. Colson's book spoke meaningfully in this vacuum because he had been at the core of the problem.

Colson told the *Christianity Today* editors that he sensed "a widespread apathy and disenchantment" which he also described as "a feeling on the part of the people that as individuals they can't do anything." Behind a decade of frustration over war, Watergate, and general domestic upheaval, he said, lay a period of about twenty-five years or more "in which people have had steadily inflated expectations of what government can do for them. Each time they are disappointed."

Colson declared, "The parallels in this country right now with the conditions in the Weimar republic in pre-Hitler days are terrifyingly vivid, in my mind. It would be the easiest thing in the world for a demagogue of the left or the right to come in and sweep the country if he had a charismatic personality, if he could promise people that he was going to solve all the ills of our society and gave them hope. If a country is desperate enough, it will rally behind a strong leader."

He called it nonsense to think that simply having a Christian in the White House would solve all the nation's problems, as some Christians seemed to be saying. But he agreed that Christians should take on more civic responsibility and become more involved in community affairs. "Government is a big part of the problem," he added, "but the other part of the problem, it seems to me, which is even more fundamental, is that every believer in this country should once a day at least be looking inside of himself, realizing that it begins with him. He needs to decide whether he has his own priorities in order, and is trying to live his own life according to what Christ teaches us. And then he needs to reach out and touch one other person with Christ's love. I think if you had a spiritual awakening in this country, it would be a lot less important whom we elect to office because the politicians still mirror the mood and the attitudes of the American people."

Colson thus suddenly became one of the world's best-known evangelical spokesmen in a way that bestirred the national conscience and showed that this was not merely warmed-over old-line fundamentalism. Many books have described conversions, but this was no derelict taking a dive at the slum mission or a teen-ager walking the sawdust trail in a revival tent. Those experiences can be spiritually authentic too, but Colson's experience was in a league that attracted attention among those who would not be interested in what happens as the result of emotional evangelistic appeals. Colson was a brilliant man who turned down a full scholarship from Harvard. He had come to know Christ, not under the influence of a hellfire sermon, but through a rational discourse. For several decades C. S. Lewis has had a profound impact upon many lives as a Christian apologist; Colson was merely the first to circulate his testimony so widely.

Colson's conversion may well represent a milestone in the maturation of evangelical Christianity in North America. One hesitates to describe this developmental stage as sophisticated and respectable unless it is understood that in this case these terms do not connote something put-on or artificial. The change is very real. It is a recognition indeed of a fuller reality, namely, that the gospel speaks to the mind as well as to the heart. The change is taking place in evangelicals' image of themselves as well as in how they are being seen from without.

Carter has the reputation of being an intelligent human being. Richard Reeves, in an article for *New York* magazine, said, "I was struck by how many national reporters believed he was the smartest politician they had ever covered. That perception was enormously helped, I think, by the performance of Southerners like Senators Ervin and Baker during the Senate Watergate hearings, which made a lot of Northern provincials realize that a cotton-mouthing accent can be connected to a first-rate mind."

In short, Carter and Colson together have helped correct an impression left by cynics who refused to associate conservative theology with thinking people.

Evangelicals, meanwhile, are adjusting their sights, perhaps unconsciously. They tend to be more patriotic in the external, traditional sense and are often accused of leaning to the political right and equating a conservative political posture with a spiritual outlook. That accusation is not true, but it is fair to say that they often side with the status quo in many facets of public policy. Watergate and the bicentennial flood of historical review have undoubtedly helped evangelicals think more seriously about what they can do to make America a better place. The combination has eventuated in signs that more evangelicals are willing to put aside, at least for a time, a measure of their political conservatism to identify with a reform-minded leader who appears to have a personal relationship with God and is not embarrassed to say so.

Evangelicals have been affected by Watergate almost to the point of disillusionment. President Nixon was greatly admired in conservative churches, both Protestant and Catholic. Despite the controversy stirred up by the White House Sunday morning services with guest speakers, many Christians felt the service showed a respect for things of the spirit that they had not before seen in a president. Nixon restricted his public utterances about divine realities to the same generalizations that had been used by politicians for many years (in his case, the reticence was attributed to his Quaker background). But under the preaching of Paul Rader, one of the better-known evangelists of the early twentieth century who was holding one of his meetings near Nixon's boyhood home, Nixon, as a youngster, had made a profession of faith and through life had given evidences of belief. When the Watergate disclosures began to spew forth, the impact upon evangelicals was little short of paralyzing.

The how-could-he-do-this-to-us reaction generated a temporary wave of cynicism among evangelicals and a short-lived return to the old feeling that politics is invariably dirty business and Christians ought to stay as far away from it as possible.

As later events would prove, Carter never let Watergate take hold of him in a negative way. He somehow foresaw that this evil would furnish the opportunity for a more authentic spiritual base in the country. He literally has used the rubble of Watergate as a foundation for a stronger Christian philosophy.

Interestingly enough, evangelicals as a whole quickly recovered their bearings. Their composite explanation of what had happened took shape around the "rationale" advanced by Jeb Magruder, White House aide and director of the 1972 Committee to Reelect the President. Magruder cited the influence of situation ethics, the notion that in the interest of love other principles sometimes may need to be suspended.

In effect, situation ethics is little more than a variation of the old idea that the end justifies the means. Indeed, Joseph Fletcher, the best-known popularizer of situation ethics says flatly that the doctrine that the end does not justify the means is "an absurd abstraction." Situation ethics grew out of existentialism to some extent although Fletcher and others deny that *situational* and *existential* are synonymous. Love is said to be the ultimate norm. Tillich was both a situationist and an existentialist, and evangelicals aware of this fact shuddered a bit when Carter quoted Tillich approvingly. One is easily ensnared in situationism; evangelicals have at times found themselves unwittingly defending its precepts in such things as Bible smuggling to Communist countries. On principle, however, evangelicals generally oppose this ethical system. Part of their problem is that they have not paid enough attention to ethics as a discipline to be discerning and able to know where they stand in light of biblical behavior patterns. Watergate jarred them into some realization of this, particularly after *Theology Today* ran a debate on whether Watergate was not situation ethics in practice and the comments were quoted elsewhere.

The post-Watergate evangelical recovery brought out a feeling long latent that evangelicals should attempt to take a stronger hand in the affairs of the country, especially through political avenues. Several significant movements arose to implement the new zeal along politically liberal as well as conservative lines. A 1975 book by James C. Hefley and Edward E. Plowman, *Washington: Christians in the Corridors of Power,* also fueled new interest. Lingering reservations about possible contamination of the faith by crude and evil political compromisers are being overridden by the 1976 sex scandals in Washington and the need they demonstrate for Judeo-Christian influence. The day calls for putting aside fears and pushing ahead with forthright action on behalf of what is true and decent.

From this standpoint, Carter has caught the attention of evangelicals simply by surfacing at the right time.

Some evangelical analysts also draw a connection between Carter and former U.S. Senator Harold Hughes of Iowa as having had a role in Carter's caucus victory in that state. Hughes's conversion, including deliverance from alcoholism, is well known in Iowa, and there is speculation that some of the respect for Hughes rubbed off on Carter as people became aware that the former Georgia governor was a brother in the faith.

Months after the Iowa campaign as I talked with Carter, he volunteered Hughes's name in discussing the term *born again.* I asked him whether the sense in which he uses *born again* is the same as that employed by Colson. Carter replied, "I presume that the phrase would be similar because I know he shares his religious faith with Senator Mark Hatfield and with others with whom I have worshiped. I know what their definition is of *born again,* and if Charles Colson's is the same, then it would be similar, yes . . . Harold Hughes is another with whom I have worshiped."

Evangelical visibility has increased even more through another best seller, the controversial marriage manual *The Total Woman.* Written by Marabel Morgan, a Florida housewife who studied philosophy at Ohio State, the book closes with a reminder that no amount of counseling measures up to the effect of regeneration. She quotes from John 3, the chapter of the Gospel from which the expression *born again* is taken. In the passage Jesus told a Jewish leader named Nicodemus that a second birth is a prerequisite for entry into the kingdom of God. These verses have been a favorite text for evangelists. Verse 16 is the most memorized portion of the Bible among evangelicals: "For God so loved the world, that he gave his only begotten Son, that whosoever believeth in him should not perish, but have everlasting life."

Many evangelicals dispute the sexual behavior advocated in *The Total Woman,* from both the liberal and the conservative perspectives, but the book does illustrate the growing ethical consciousness among evangelicals, the desire to translate biblical precepts into the specifics of everyday behavior. What exactly does God want from me in my behavior, in my work, and in my overall goals? A lot of Carter's thinking on this score came out during the primary campaign, and evangelicals were readily identifying with it, especially in regard to their jobs.

Carter's father died of cancer at a relatively early age; that happened in 1953, and Jimmy won release from the service to go back to Plains where he and his family began to rethink their concept of vocation. Rosalynn strongly opposed Jimmy's leaving the service but went along and then helped him get started in business. It was a tough decision for Carter himself because his goal had been to become chief of naval operations. He and Rosalynn got an apartment in a new federally funded public housing project in Plains and went to the local bank for a loan, only to be refused. Fortunately they had saved some money while Jimmy was in the navy, so they started growing certified seed peanuts. The 1954 growing season turned out to be one of the worst in Georgia history because of a drought. Carter's total profit for the first year was less than two hundred dollars.

He also sold fertilizer in 100- and 200-pound bags, often loading the bags himself. Farming was changing, and Carter had forgotten a lot. He had plenty of studying to do along with his physical labors.

Carter had left the navy while wondering whether with only one life to spend one should use it to engage in war, "even if I could rationalize it as the prevention of war," as he told a reporter. Back in Plains and being in business but beginning to think of politics, the question of how best to use time here on earth was cropping up again.

Similar questions were being raised by evangelicals throughout North America, along with the related issue of how the Christian faith should affect work. Groups of evangelical doctors, lawyers, librarians, historians, artists, and others formed national organizations in the '50s and '60s to confront these questions.

J. Herbert Gilmore explored the relationship of worship and work in *When Love Prevails: A Pastor Speaks to a Church in Crisis:* "When a person's inner life seems shallow, his devotion as refreshing as a dried-up pond, it is often an indication that there has been no expression of his Christian faith in creative service. And when a person becomes so exhausted in his effort that he is ready to quit, it is a good indication that he has not fed his spirit with genuine prayer, meditation, and worship. When a man cultivates the inner life, which the five foolish virgins did not do, then he has that desire to express it in moral action. Then his moral action takes on fire, and direction, and purpose, and he comes back again to replenish his own lamp. I cannot overemphasize the truth that the Christian life must always be lived in the tension of worship and work."

Would it not be reasonable to conclude that in 1976 many evangelicals looking at the life of Carter will identify with his effort to translate belief into action, especially in the context of vocation?

Christian young people, wanting desperately to change the world, have frequently agonized over vocation, asking themselves particularly whether there are key vocations through which to exert a great example and to extend healing balms to the ills of society. Intelligent young believers know it is not enough to hope and pray and sing and contribute money for the advancement of God's kingdom.

In what was probably the most penetrating interview of Carter during the primary campaign, Bill Moyers asked Carter, "What drives you?"

Carter replied, "I feel like I have one life to live. I feel that God wants me to do the best I can with it. And that's quite often my major prayer. Let me live my life so that it will be meaningful.

And I enjoy attacking difficult problems and . . . answering the difficult questions and the meticulous organization of a complicated effort."

Moyers asked Carter how he knew God's will, and Carter answered that he prays frequently. "When I have a sense of peace and just self-assurance—I don't know where it comes from—that what I'm doing is the right thing, I assume, maybe in an unwarranted way, that that's doing God's will."

After World War II a young bus driver became a Christian and felt impelled to enter the ministry. He went to his pastor for counsel and was told to forget the idea and to stick to bus driving. He made the approach repeatedly with the same result. Finally he went again to the pastor and exclaimed, "Look, God has called me to preach. I've *got* to preach." Whereupon the wise old pastor declared, "That's what I've been waiting to hear you say. Now you're ready to apply for training." The bus driver eventually became pastor of that church, and it thrived under his ministry.

For many people, God's call is not that apparent or compelling. The vocational decision is not made quickly or easily. God's call comes not in one loud shout but in a long series of barely discernible whispers. We pray for guidance, and he makes us work for the answer. Such work has often taken the form of prevocational involvement wherein the student tries out various fields in part-time work.

In one sense Carter had a hard time finding his niche; in another sense his experience in assorted pursuits prepared him for work in which a broad, interdisciplinary understanding is an incomparable asset.

Evangelicals have not yet developed a substantial theology of vocation appropriate to modern needs, and good literature on the subject is lean. The best introduction is "The Christian View of Work," a chapter in Carl F. H. Henry's *Aspects of Christian*

Social Ethics. Christian counselors have had to settle for merely helping bring the widest possible picture into focus.

The basic vocational decision which faces Christians in modern times is whether to opt for "full-time Christian service" or "secular" work. This dichotomy apparently originated with the pietists who after the Reformation drifted back to the traditional Roman Catholic distinction between the priesthood and the laity. But the trend has been away from such sharp separation, partly for theological reasons, partly because there is greater specialization of tasks even in church-related vocations, and partly because of the increasing recognition that every occupation should have a biblical dimension. It used to be, for example, that Bible-school graduates were recruited for "general missionary work." Today they go to foreign countries as doctors, linguists, teachers, pilots, radio technicians—yet as evangelists as well. Christians now see more clearly that the lay person is also a minister (which is why some churches prefer the term *pastor* to *minister*). The Christian cannot discharge his or her biblical responsibility simply by contributing to the salaries of underpaid "professional Christians." The work of God must be carried out in the context of all kinds of careers and human activity.

Carter once argued with a clergyman over vocation. "One year during our annual revival services at our church in Plains," he recalled, "the visiting minister stayed for the week in my mother's home. After the evening service, he and I were discussing public service in its many possible forms. During the conversation I told him that I was considering running for public office. The Georgia Senate was being reapportioned, and for the first time would have a permanent membership with substantive and continuing responsibilities. The pastor was surprised that I would consider going into politics, and strongly advised me not to become involved in such a discredited profession. We had a rather heated argument, and he finally asked, 'If you want to be of service to other people, why don't you go into the ministry or into some honorable social service work?' On the spur of the moment I retorted, 'How would you like to be the pastor of a church with 80,000 members?' He finally admitted that it was possible to stay honest and at the same time minister to the needs of the 80,000 citizens of the 14th Senate district."

When Carter became governor, Alice Murray, religion writer for the *Atlanta Constitution,* quoted him as saying, "I see every legitimate concern of government as a legitimate concern of Christians. I have considered myself in 'full-time Christian service' every day I have been governor."

The Scripture passage perhaps most directly relevant to lifework is found in the Apostle Paul's first letter to the church at Corinth. It emphasizes neither gifts nor circumstances but calling. "Let every one lead the life which the Lord has assigned to him, and in which God has called him. This is my rule in all the churches. Was any one at the time of his call already circumcised? Let him not seek to remove the marks of circumcision. Was any one at the time of his call uncircumcised? Let him not seek circumcision. For neither circumcision counts for anything nor uncircumcision, but keeping the commandments of God. Every one should remain in the state in which he was called. Were you a slave when called? Never mind. But if you can gain your freedom, avail yourself of the opportunity. For he who was called in the Lord as a slave is a freedman of the Lord. Likewise he who was free when called is a slave of Christ. You were bought with a price; do not become slaves of men. So, brethren, in whatever state each was called, there let him remain with God" (1 Cor. 7:17–24, *Revised Standard Version*).

On the basis of this passage, Luther expounded his great doctrine of the priesthood of all believers, declaring that the divine calling was not limited to the clergy. He saw every vocation as an avenue of divine service. This is a tremendous truth, but Luther may have gotten a bit carried away in suggesting at one point that people should therefore be discouraged from striving for influential office because "sitting at the top is no fun. . . . It entails so much labor and displeasure that he who is sensible will make no great attempt to attain the position."

Reporter Murray quoted Carter as saying that his time as governor broadened his concepts and strengthened his faith and that "it makes me know a little more about the priesthood of believers and about the Lordship of Christ." He observed that offering simplistic solutions for complicated problems is no longer tenable.

Calvin built on Luther, urging Christians to take a more dynamic view of their vocations. As Henry J. Ryskamp has put it, "Luther was content with the idea that men should not neglect to serve God *in* their vocations," whereas Calvin "exhorted his readers and followers to serve God *through* their vocations." Evangelicals have been sensing that the challenge is not just to do secular jobs well and honestly but to find special divine purpose and biblical dimensions in them that would not occur to the unbeliever. Why echo secular patterns and attitudes that were developed from views alien to or at odds with Christianity?

There is enough ambiguity about 1 Corinthians 7:9–24 (especially v. 21, which is rendered in contradictory ways even in modern translations) that one ought not try to build an airtight case on it alone. Some liberal scholars tend to dismiss Paul's remarks here as just another manifestation of his fatalism, his supposed feeling that the world was soon going to end, so Christians might as well stick with what they were doing. But most evangelical New Testament scholars feel Paul is urging Christians to stay in the jobs they were doing before they became Christians.

Perhaps he is suggesting that by staying there they become the salt of the earth, permeating society for the sake of God's righteousness. Indeed, Paul may be saying only that one ought not break previous commitments and obligations in order to take up a new vocation after conversion.

For a number of years prior to 1976, the country had been undergoing an acute case of nostalgia. Demand for antiques was one of the most obvious aspects of the trend, along with the popularity of colonial furniture. There was growing interest in folk craft, in doing all kinds of things in natural, old-fashioned ways. The American psyche was realizing that the simpler days brought a gratification that had been missing under the intense preoccupation with modern technology. Producers of television dramas responded to the yearning; programs rooted in nostalgia, like "The Waltons," got high ratings. Would it not be simply a matter of time until there was also an awakening of interest in the *values* of bygone days? A pair of clean-cut Mormon teen-agers, Donny and Marie Osmond, made an instant hit with a Friday night prime-time show that not only reenacted old scenes but featured humor remarkably devoid of the off-color themes exploited by most other top programs.

Attention to ethics, life-style, and sense of purpose was not limited to evangelicals. American society in general appeared to be recognizing a basic need to distinguish right from wrong. Sputnik produced a new scientific and technological consciousness that was promptly implemented in education and industry. Watergate should have roused the country much more than it did to the ethical dimensions of its life together. There has been some soul-searching but too little intensive follow-up in the public schools. Partly because of the Supreme Court's ban on religious exercises, public schools have been reluctant to engage in value training.

Honesty is needed not only in government but everywhere else. Evangelicals have been trying to get that message across, but ethics has been a terribly neglected discipline. Most people never have a course in it unless they go to college. Even in higher education, the study of ethics is undertaken only a by relative handful. Many attain advanced degrees without even a smattering of it.

Medical ethics has received considerable attention in recent years, but progress at that level will be slow until better foundations are laid.

Evangelicals are beginning to press the argument that instruction in right versus wrong is as important to social order and stability as training in the use of language. True, ethics in a way permeates or is at least touched upon in a number of school subjects, but only concentration is going to achieve results. And parents can be expected to resist programs such as sex education until there is value orientation.

Traditionally, the home and the church have been relied upon to instill in children a set of behavioral standards. Unfortunately, many parents and preachers stress doctrinal beliefs and personal spiritual and mental well-being without relating much to everyday conduct.

Doctrine is certainly a prerequisite to the Christian faith, but to relegate ethics to secondary consideration is to shortchange the biblical message. The whole idea behind Christian conversion or regeneration is that it makes one a new person morally. The Apostle Paul is often quoted telling the church at Corinth that "if anyone is in Christ, he is a new creation."

Ethical reticence on the part of Christians in the past may have been partly attributable to their respect for the religious liberties of others. Responsible Christians understand that in a pluralistic society they cannot impose their code upon unwilling subjects.

They do desire a voice in determining the code and ask that it respect their views. What Christians and non-Christians together should fear is the current failure to teach *any* ethical consensus.

One way in which Carter has spoken to the revival of old values is his espousal of plain hard work. "I believe in the work ethic," he said flatly. He reiterated this belief to labor groups, to businessmen's meetings, and to gatherings of farmers. The statement appeared as the first item in a widely distributed piece of campaign literature.

That element came on the heels of talk about the problems of a leisure society and discussion of four-day workweeks. Did it signal a reversal? Was Carter detecting that more leisure is *not* what the country wants, that perhaps a heightened sense of responsibility is needed to deal with the frequently cited problem of boredom?

Whatever is happening in America in 1976, it is clear that a substantial element in the country is striving to get away from materialism and is moving toward renewed respect for things that though intangible are real. Some are daring to hope that the back-to-nature movement brought on by ecological concerns might go so far as to embrace a renewal of natural law and natural theology, the idea that God has placed self-revealing principles in the created universe. Evidence that this actually might be happening came in the publication of a book which called for recognition that there is evil in the world that needs to be dealt with. The book *Whatever Became of Sin?* was written by a distinguished psychiatrist, Karl Menninger, to counter the widely held opinion that no realities automatically entail guilt. Christians welcomed the work because they regard sin as humanity's basic problem which, when denied, not only cancels out religion but makes true moral progress impossible. There is no way to deal with evil if you are not aware of it.

The works of Malcolm Muggeridge and Alexander Solzhenitzyn have further sensitized the reading public in the direction of Christian thinking. Muggeridge, the incomparably witty British writer who so long reflected skepticism, in his sunset years turned his pen to the praise of Christ. Solzhenitzyn, with his thunderingly eloquent critique of détente, has confirmed the fears of many, including evangelicals. Carter calls for much more careful bargaining with Communist countries.

Even in the formal academic ranks there is a move toward conservatism. A number of theologians issued the so-called Hartford Declaration, attempting to set boundaries for theological speculations and thus avoid far-out exercises such as the death-of-God fad.

Undoubtedly, Carter has gotten a lift too from the rise of the New South and the greater respect being shown people living below the Mason-Dixon line by residents of other parts of the country. Black people are still a long way from equality in the nation's third century, but most are aware that they have come a long way. The North is having its own problems with busing and with other racially related matters and is no longer in a position to be judgmental.

While the South has gained stature and thus Carter is more acceptable than a Southerner might have been twenty years ago, another kind of regionalism has developed that enhances him even more. Growing distrust and dislike of the so-called Eastern elite is being repeatedly expressed. Carter won many primary votes by underscoring the fact that he is not a part of that establishment. He charged over and over that federal officials have become too removed from the people, and he emphasized his inclination to be as close to the grass roots as possible. He demonstrated this alignment by dropping in on a wide variety of ethnic affairs and mingling with ordinary folks at every opportunity. Considering that he entered virtually all the primaries and campaigned hard in each one, there is no doubt that he has shaken more hands than any other presidential candidate in American history.

Carter did not suddenly become an advocate of all the new movements, but he did take what he thought were the best elements out of a number of them. The result might be called the Carter composite or the Carter coalition. It is literally a people's agenda from which he has taken his issues. He has tried harder than any other candidate to find out what is bothering people the most, and he has built his campaign program accordingly. He does not give answers that please everyone, but he reflects a confidence in being conscious of people's deepest concerns and building upon them.

The people who voted in the 1976 primaries showed a clear preference for Carter's ethical concern and his approach to dealing with issues. Some figured that politicians don't keep their promises anyway, so why be intent on learning exactly what candidates say they will do. After all, Kennedy won the election citing a "missile gap" that did not exist, Johnson was the peace candidate telling Asian boys it was their war and not America's, and Nixon went into office saying he was bringing the country together.

Less cynical voters identify with Carter when they conclude that the issues issue is not that he is evading questions but that he is not dealing with matters his opponents regard as key questions. Carter's field work has convinced him that he knows more about the things people care about than other politicians who tend to take their cues from the media and from lobbyists.

Carter says he was questioned more about abortion during the primary campaign than about any other one subject. In Iowa, because of a heavy Catholic population and because Protestants in the state tend to be more conservative, the abortion issue was paramount.

Carter says consistently that he personally opposes abortion. He is unwilling, however, to support constitutional amendments to overturn the U.S. Supreme Court's 1973 ruling which struck down state laws prohibiting abortions during the first thirteen weeks of pregnancy. Carter argues that government should discourage abortion, through legislation or administrative decree, within the confines of the court decision. He proposes "better education, better family planning, making better contraceptive devices available and providing for better adoption procedures to minimize abortion."

During the Iowa primary campaign, columnists Rowland Evans and Robert Novak wrote: "Carter's image here resembles former Senator Harold Hughes, one of Iowa's most popular figures: self-made man, devout Christian, and—what is new for Carter—foreign policy dove. That image has helped Carter build from scratch a coalition ranging from the progressive United Auto Workers to Iowa's most conservative Democrats."

Carter won only 27.6 percent of the vote in Iowa, but the total was more than that of any other candidate. Moreover, said *Newsweek*, "as an early litmus test of candidate credibility" the caucuses "had thrust a fresh new face into the forefront of Presidential speculation."

Many Catholics as well as Protestants are frankly disappointed that Carter does not take a stronger stand against abortion itself. Christians differ on the morality of abortion because the Bible says little about it. They do not differ on the responsibility a Christian has to back up words with deeds. After the Democratic platform committee influenced by the Carter staff adopted a plank against a human life amendment to the Constitution, Dr. Mildred F. Jefferson, the black woman surgeon from Boston who serves as president of the National Right to Life Committee, put the question bluntly:

"Candidate Carter must now tell the 40 million evangelical Christians exactly what his position on abortion means. His opposition to a Human Life Amendment which would protect the life of the unborn child is not reasonable for a candidate who is running for President in a moral crusade. If he is running for President as a Christian crusader and cannot recognize the moral issues in abortion, he is misleading the people and he is a hypocrite. If he recognizes the moral wrong of abortion and refuses to try to correct it, then he is morally bankrupt and he does not deserve the votes of the believing people."

Carter won Iowa, and his moderate stand on abortion may have been pivotal, but did it commit him to back off later when national embarrassment was at stake?

5

For Outsiders . . .

DESPITE THE new American openness toward many of the things Carter represents, he still came on as an alien. At no time was this more evident than during a twenty-four-hour visit to Washington just before the Winston-Salem episode.

Media people got in free. So did prospective convention delegates. Most of the rest of the crowd in the elegant little Georgetown row house had paid a hundred dollars each to hail the conquering hero or at least to experience briefly his mystical presence. Together they formed wall-to-wall people, but few complained of the crush. The bulk of the crowd were admirers of the honored guest savoring an in-person close-up of what was becoming the most celebrated smile since Dwight Eisenhower and the most caricatured teeth in political history.

Between hugs and handshakes Jimmy Carter inched his way toward the north end of the living room where TV crews awaited his word for Washington.

Fund-raising receptions are common to politics, but this one was different for Carter because it was in Washington, and Carter had been giving Washington a working-over that set precedents even for politicians.

The opening page of the Carter autobiography asks, "*Does* our government in Washington now represent accurately what the American people are, or what we ought to be?" The answer, he said, is a clear no.

In his first fund-raising letter, after announcing his presidential candidacy, Carter argued that "people are disillusioned with officials in Washington. They are looking for a new face, a new leader whose ideas work." He kept up the barrage during more than two thousand speeches of his primary campaign. In the last one, delivered at a Cherry Hill, New Jersey, shopping mall, Carter described the "mess in Washington" with a long string of stinging adjectives: horrible, bloated, confused, overlapping, wasteful, inefficient, ineffective, unmanageable, insensitive, and bureaucratic.

Regional politicians aspiring to national office invariably attack the federal government, but they usually limit their verbal fire to the shortcomings of the other party. Carter's accusations at least implicitly transcended the partisan line. Although he emphasized deficiencies in the Republican-controlled executive branch, he did it in such a way that his hearers usually inferred that the legislative and even the judicial branches were also being implicated.

"There is no clear vision of what is to be accomplished," Carter had said in launching his candidacy. "Everyone struggles for temporary advantage, and there is no way to monitor how effectively services are delivered."

Now the prosecutor had come to the locale of the crime. Some at the reception may have wondered whether at least indirectly they would be put on the spot as witnesses, if not as aiders or abettors. By and large, however, they were not Washington political types, according to *Washington Post* columnist Richard Cohen. In a subsequent spoof he wrote that he had come to the reception to "look the man in the eye and see if I was suddenly seized with a desire to run as a Carter delegate. This was going to be the moment of truth—twice-born Christian vs. Bar Mitzvah boy with cheek."

Cohen observed that the crowd was largely men and women he had never seen before. He did recognize his son's pediatrician, a former school board member, and a state senator from Maryland who was a farmer.

Cohen wrote in mock derision that Carter "was breaking the rules" of the Eastern political establishment because he was an outsider. "Washington is accustomed to keeping the presidency in the area. Italians feel somewhat the same way about the papacy. It saves on moving costs. We smile with condescension whenever Virginia proclaims itself the Mother of Presidents. . . . The real mother of presidents, we know, is the Spring Valley section of Washington." Richard Nixon and Lyndon Johnson lived in Spring Valley prior to their ascent to the White House. Like Georgetown, Spring Valley lies in the northwest section of Washington.

Jack W. Germond of the *Washington Star* said on a more serious note that even before the start of the primaries Carter was alien "partly because he comes on so strong, so implacably self-assured and apparently independent of the system. To conventional politicians he is a threatening outsider, and they are clearly outraged at his attempts to pass himself off as just folks from Plains, Georgia, when they have discovered he knows many of their best tricks."

Germond cited the plays of Tennessee Williams, in which the protagonist is often a foreign presence, sometimes a Sicilian. His introduction of a different ethic to the community arouses all the traumatic dislocations of personal and social relationships that make the drama. "In the campaign of 1976," Germond declared, "Jimmy Carter is a political Sicilian."

Evangelicals, on the whole, have also been playing the outsider role. When Carter came along, they got the message that he knew better than anyone else of comparable stature that they were out there.

It was self-symptomatic that a Roman Catholic, a layman at that though a philosopher, surfaced the fact publicly. In a commentary published in the *Washington Post* in early spring 1976 and widely quoted thereafter, Michael Novak wrote: "There is a hidden religious power base in American culture which our secular biases prevent many of us from noticing. Jimmy Carter has found it.

"Usually in America, when we say 'Protestant,' we think of slender white New England churches. We think of Puritans; of Exeter, Andover and Groton; of Yale Divinity School and Riverside Church. We mean our Pilgrim forefathers. We think of sobriety, strictness, severity, hard work.

"Most of this is wrong. Overwhelming numbers of Protestants in the United States are evangelicals, fresh from an experience of conversion, who speak easily of 'fellowship,' 'tenderness,' 'conversion,' and 'love.'

"The most understated demographic reality in the United States is the huge number of evangelical Protestants, Jimmy Carter's natural constituency."

Novak goes on with some description of evangelicals, then adds: "Not all politicians, even when they try, can touch the inner springs of this evangelical sensibility. When Richard Nixon went to Nashville [sic], it felt wrong. When he spoke to friendly crowds in North Carolina, he came somehow as a stranger, affirming words that weren't his native tongue. But when Jimmy Carter speaks, millions of Protestant Americans experience a sudden smack of recognition. He's for real." Novak was referring to Nixon's 1970 visit to a Billy Graham rally in Knoxville.

Novak continues: "On a national stage, resistance to Carter is not so much because those in other symbol systems are 'prejudiced against Southerners' or are afraid 'they don't own Jimmy.' Rather, the source of discomfort is that they do not know at first hand the pressures that shaped him, his inner demons and his inner angels. They can't confidently imagine scenarios of various pressures upon him and predict how he will act. He is, from his point of view, an outsider breaking in on their world. But they are, from their point of view, outsiders who can't quite understand what makes him tick.

"The tragedy of American pluralism is that there are many 'outsiders' in American public life—a vast horde of strong individuals from various traditions who have never exercised control over the presidential (and other national) symbol systems: blacks, women of various cultures, Latinos, but also Poles, Italians, Jews, Japanese, Scandinavians and many others. Each takes a certain getting used to. . . .

"Blacks more than Catholics and Jews are familiar with the Carter symbolic style; they, too, are evangelical, Protestant and Southern in tradition."

Novak was saying that the evangelical ethos had been there for quite a while but that few had ever taken notice.

Whether "symbolic style" or something else, Carter was sensing what a veteran Washington pundit saw, that the "bulk of voters want the federal government to be run in a tidier, more human fashion, and they would prefer someone who hasn't been in the bureaucracy to be in charge." Carter has emphasized his lack of experience as an elected national official.

The typical opening lines of a Carter primary speech were, "I'm not from Washington [applause]. I'm not a lawyer [applause]. I think this is the time for someone outside of Washington about my age." He told the *New York Times* in late February that the Georgetown-Chevy Chase dinner-party crowd feared "that someone who is not their candidate might actually become the next president."

In deed as well as in word, Carter demonstrated aloofness to Washington. He placed his national campaign headquarters in Atlanta rather than in Washington although a subservient regional office was opened in the capital. During the primary, inquiries of any consequence were always referred to Atlanta; Washington campaign workers professed ignorance of where their man happened to be on a particular day.

British-born Dr. Peter Bourne, a psychiatrist and energetic Carter supporter moved from Atlanta in 1973 to supervise Washington-area affairs from an upper-floor suite in an old but tidy office building at Twentieth and P Streets. The structure overlooks DuPont Circle, favorite haunt of Vietnam-era dissenters of which Bourne was one. Reportedly, Carter aides tried unsuccessfully to reduce Bourne's role following the primaries.

Carter even swam against the tide in his design of campaign literature. Green ink displaced the traditional red, white, and blue, bicentennial year notwithstanding.

Carter's national primary headquarters were located along Atlanta's legendary Peachtree thoroughfare. One of the three buildings housing the Carter workers was located next door to an office building at 1776 Peachtree which was occupied by a regional office of the General Services Administration. Carter campaigners did manage to get a post office box in Atlanta numbered 1776.

Carter tried some course correction so as not to make it appear that he was about to dismantle Washington and cart it off to

Atlanta. "I've never expressed deliberately any anti-Washington feeling or any antigovernment feeling," he told Moyers. "When, as Truman said, you know, people say I'm giving them hell, but when I tell the truth, they think truth is hell." With a little better syntax, Carter added, "I never have said I wanted a small government. I want one that, when it performs a function, does it well . . . in the ways that alleviate the problems of those who have not had an adequate voice in the past."

Carter obviously does not feel that evangelicals are the only outsiders. Out of understandable reticence he has never explicitly talked much about evangelicals as such, but he has pounded away at the theme that political leaders have been isolated from the people. "They have made decisions from an ivory tower," he said at the National Press Club. "Few have ever seen personally the direct impact of government programs involving welfare, prisons, mental institutions, unemployment, school busing or public housing. Our people feel that they have little access to the core of government and little influence with elected officials."

Carter was an outsider even in his own Democratic party. He was a political alien, as one observer put it, with no long history of association with any element of the party—not labor, or the academic community, or the antiwar movement, or big-city machines, or Congress.

Much speculation has been expressed about the outsider image. Ronald Reagan and even President Ford are not exactly in the mainstream. Ford is a congressional veteran, but mostly as part of the losing side because as a Republican in the House he was in a perpetual minority. Governor Jerry Brown's strong showing came partly because of his outsider role.

Evangelicals have been outsiders, not only in American society as a whole, but in the structured religious life of the country. By choice, most have had little participation in or association with the leadership of major denominations or the National Council of Churches. For decades, evangelical scholars were almost systematically excluded from key academic appointments. They were seldom quoted in serious books or periodicals J. Gresham Machen of Princeton, the leading fundamentalist thinker of the first half of the twentieth century, has been all but gnored despite several great works; Walter Lippmann was th exception who recognized Machen in the fundamentalist-modernist controversy, crediting him with having developed "the bes popular argument produced by either side."

Carter has taken some ribbing about his antiestablishment posture although it has been more along the lines of good humor than in the context of the sarcasm and ridicule heaped upon early fundamentalists. Columnist Russell Baker, quoting from a mythical 1976 edition of "The Modern Political Dictionary," defined Washington as "a metropolis of the mid-Atlantic region which is so detestable and odious to out-of-office politicians that they spend millions of dollars, risk destruction of their marriages, and labor for years to fulfill their dreams of being sent there." Baker described the phrase "hunger for new faces" as "political jargon pertaining to a widely perceived public urge to place its most difficult problems in inexperienced hands. Thus, e.g., a voter who insists that his gall bladder be removed by a freshman medical student instead of a hospital chief-of-surgery, is said to have a 'hunger for new faces.' "

The new face nonetheless saw fit to appear in Washington in light of the upcoming primary there and in adjacent Maryland. He also had his eye on nearby Virginia where party caucuses would soon commit convention delegates. A *Post* story noted, "Some people say Washington isn't the United States and Jimmy Carter often says Georgetown isn't either. Yet Georgetown is where Carter could be found the last two nights, despite his jabs at the Chevy Chase-Georgetown establishment and its 'non-elected professional politicians.' "

The Georgetown fund-raising reception took place as primary polls were closing in Illinois, where Carter had been for part of the day before. He had flown to Washington and a dinner the previous night at the Georgetown home of columnist Clayton Fritchey. With them were such celebrities as former defense secretary Clark Clifford, Common Cause leader John Gardner, CBS-TV commentator Eric Sevareid, and *Post* publisher Katharine Graham. *Newsweek* reported on the event, "Carter came early, stayed late and was scrupulously low-key and correct, moving from one table to another to share oysters, pink lamb and vanilla soufflé with the high-powered guests who wanted to see where he stood." The next day Carter showed up at meetings with leaders of the nationwide municipal workers union, the congressional black caucus, and editors of the *Post.*

These were closed meetings, and most who came away were reluctant to commit themselves on Carter. But Clark Clifford was reported as saying he had been "gratified that he [Carter] seems knowledgeable" on foreign policy. "His views are . . . moderate and I think really perceptive." Another guest was described as being impressed by "how open and specific Carter was on issues."

Ironically enough, while Carter was in Washington, Senator Frank Church was in the Georgetown home of Senator Claiborne Pell announcing his presidential candidacy "because I believe the issues are not being discussed."

Carter's Tuesday reception was held at the home of Smith Bagley, an heir of the Reynolds Tobacco Company. Bagley and his family rent the house on 28th Street once owned by Teddy Kennedy. The façade of the red-brick two-story structure with blue shutters features a curved bay-window-like protrusion from ground to roof. Out of the narrow front yard a woody vine rises up the wall as if threatening to strangle the rain spouts. The house is situated in the northeast corner of Georgetown, within and near the 1792 boundary of what was the Evermay estate. The estate land had been purchased with the proceeds from the sale of acreage a mile or two to the east, including part of the White House grounds and Lafayette Square.

Although Georgetown is the prestigious area where many Washington greats make their home, in the '60s and '70s it has also been a rendezvous point for antiestablishment young people. The business area is a curious blend of high-price shops and fancy restaurants and stores catering to those on the natural kick. The Georgetown sector of Washington is a limited geographical area lying along the Potomac River west of Rock Creek. Between the river and M Street, which runs roughly parallel to it, the buildings are occupied mostly by small businesses of varying sorts, including some light industry. North of M Street lies the main residential concentration of row houses—old but undergoing restoration—overgrown with magnolias and boxwoods and laced with brick sidewalks conducive to ankle sprains. To the west is the campus of Georgetown University, operated by the Jesuits and dating back to 1789.

The Bagleys were obliged to keep open their front door to accommodate the comings and goings of Carter viewers. Spring arrived early in the nation's capital in 1976, with thermometers stretching toward ninety by the latter part of February. The famed cherry blossoms were nearly at their peak by the ides of March when a blustery spell again bared the trees. Between one and three inches of snow had been forecast for Carter's arrival, but none fell. Instead there were sporadic light showers with winds gusting to fifty miles an hour.

There were not many evangelicals to show their theological colors at the reception, but one devout young man gave Carter a copy of a Pentecostal-oriented tabloid later used by the presidential aspirant to spread across a finely finished bench which he mounted to address the gathering.

Carter's comments were anticlimactically brief. He again denied being anti-Washington. The basic American system is still something to be thankful for, he said. He asked his supporters not to get discouraged over primary losses, and like a radio or television evangelist signing off, he invited people to write him. With that he scurried off to New York, where that same evening he surveyed his Illinois primary victory on CBS television as a guest of Walter Cronkite.

America has a history of making room for outsiders when they assert themselves, and in microcosm, Georgetown, with haven for the more-idealistic young, is like that.

For many people, Carter's Deep South origin is enough to make him an outsider. Southerners have long influenced Washington, but the most common representation of them as lawmakers is that of the senator drawling away to a high emotional pitch. Carter's accent is decidedly Southern, but his forceful oratory is relatively low-key. Part of the preparation for his candidacy was some counsel from Dr. Hubert Vance Taylor at the Protestant Radio and Television Center in Atlanta.

Carter's tie to farm life has also worked toward his outsider image although in recent years ecological concerns, hunger alarms, and a new yearning for the great outdoors have brought agricultural workers back into the good graces of city dwellers. Prior to this latest reversal, city life was praised to the point that the farmer was rarely mentioned, and then only in disparaging terms. For a period even theologians looked condescendingly at Bible times because of the agrarian orientation; Scripture was discounted because it seemed irrelevant to industrialized society. The recovery of respect for farm life still has a way to go, and many minds still count Carter's rural background a decided liability. (Carter likes to point to the bit of irony that Plains has about the same population density as Atlanta: about eight hundred people to the square mile.)

One person who has had a great influence on Carter has also been an outsider. The two originally met in Washington! Carter did not have a slogan during his primary campaign, but he came close in the frequency with which he cited the question, Why not the best? It's the title of his autobiography, and he got it from being interviewed by the father of this country's nuclear submarine fleet, Hyman G. Rickover.

Rickover, a legend in his time, has acquired a reputation for a wide range of idiosyncrasies. One of his quirks has been to subject prospective employees to humiliating interviews. He has insisted on talking beforehand to everyone being considered for a job of any consequence in the nuclear submarine program. Thousands have undergone the grilling. He might ask them to sing a solo on the spot or to tell how they proposed marriage (he has been known to get in touch with the spouse to verify the account). No one ever forgets being with Rickover, and the impact on Carter was considerable.

Rickover let Carter choose whatever subject he thought he was most conversant with, then promptly showed the young officer how little he knew about it. "Finally," Carter recalls, "he asked me a question and I thought I could redeem myself." Rickover wanted to know his class standing at Annapolis, and Carter proudly replied that he had been fifty-ninth out of 829. Then the deflating follow-up, "Did you do your best?" Well, how many of us could honestly answer that kind of question affirmatively? So Carter said no, and Rickover shot back, "Why not?" The question has been ringing in Carter's ears ever since.

Carter got the job nevertheless, and his dealings with Rickover thereafter were unparalleled learning experiences. Rickover, though eccentric and seemingly unable ever to pay anyone a compliment, is a model of hard work, efficiency, and perseverance. No one in Washington is better known for challenging bureaucratic red tape to get jobs done. He has become an expert at getting past foot-dragging superiors. His lack of tact would have cost most military men their promotions, and it almost did his: special legislation by Congress kept Rickover working.

Although Carter has retained a priority on diplomacy, there is no doubt that Rickover's impatience with poor management practices rubbed off on him. "As a full admiral responsible for naval nuclear propulsion, Rickover has had twenty-one intermediate authorities between him and the Secretary of Defense," Carter wrote in his autobiography. "Each of the twenty-one could veto or delay a proposal, but none could give final approval." In effect, Rickover has always been a Washington outsider who got his way only because there was respect for his ability and a sense of urgency about the need for the end product.

Hardly anyone has dared to quibble with Rickover for the record. In fact, only with the rise of Carter has the voice of dissent finally been heard in public. A dispute over cost overruns apparently triggered it. Gordon W. Rule, a navy procurement official, told a group of shipbuilders in early 1976 that Rickover's methods are "arrogant, autocratic and totally foreign to our American concepts of simple decency and fairness."

It takes some doing for Carter to be assertive. Those closest to him and his wife say they both tend to be shy by nature, and the candidate concedes that dealing with people does not come as readily to him as it seems to for many people. Carter interacts in the spotlight more out of a sense of duty and responsibility than out of sheer pleasure. Some might consider his personality that of a loner, but it is rather that dealing with people gratifies him mentally and intellectually rather than physically and emotionally.

The *Economist of London* has noted that following the 1968 Democratic National Convention massive surveys were conducted on Middle America. Analyses of them showed that "the political parties were losing their grip, the loyalties that had supported them were dissolving wholesale, the leaders were discredited, the followers estranged. In short, if new leaders appeared they would find the doors open. One who heard the message was Jimmy Carter . . ."

When the roll call was being taken at the 1976 Democratic National Convention which would choose Jimmy Carter as presidential nominee for the party, the delegate reporting the vote from Nebraska noted that his was the state of William Jennings Bryan. It is hard to compare Carter or even to draw approximate parallels between him and figures of the past. Nevertheless, Carter is somewhat reminiscent of Bryan, and not only because of the latter's outspoken evangelical views. Carter's outsider image recalls Bryan more than any other feature despite the fa t that Bryan was called the "peerless leader" of the Democratic party and "the Great Commoner." He represented the West against conservative interests in the East. Actually, Bryan was born in Salem, Illinois (the name *Salem* is derived from the Hebrew *shalom*, which is roughly translated "peace" and is fairly common as an American town name, not to mention Jeru*salem*).

Bryan has undergone considerable restudy in recent years. Students of his life and work are beginning to see that his positive achievements far outweigh the negative image stemming from the infamous Scopes trial. Bryan, in fact, died a few days after the trial ended.

According to Robert D. Linder, professor of history at Kansas Sate University, Bryan's personal and political reputation is being restored, and evangelicals are rediscovering a respected hero of the faith.

"Bryan had long been known as an outspoken champion of the Christian faith," Linder wrote in a *Christianity Today* article. "A testifying Presbyterian, he was unabashed in his stand for evangelical Christianity and the application of Christian principles to politics. Bryan . . . three-time Democratic presidential nominee, was something of an American folk hero especially in rural America. As a man of impeccable morality and Christian idealism he was a 'shining knight' of the progressive era of American history."

It surprises some people to learn that a fundamentalist like Bryan was held in high esteem by a wide spectrum of people. Felix Frankfurter, the distinguished former Supreme Court justice, has spoken of his youthful devotion to Bryan in glowing terms. Said Frankfurter, "If you recall the kind of excitement that tousled-hair Wendell Willkie stirred, suddenly somebody emerged, William Jennings Bryan emerged that way for me."

Bryan was a great orator of the old tradition. In a debate over the free-silver plank at the 1896 Democratic National Convention, he delivered what is probably the most famous oration ever made before an American political convention: "Having behind us the producing masses of this nation and the world, supported by the commercial interests, the laboring interests, and the toilers everywhere, we will answer their demand for a gold standard by saying to them: You shall not press down upon the brow of labor this crown of thorns, you shall not crucify mankind upon a cross of gold." The speech won for him the presidential nomination at the age of thirty-six.

It is unfair and unfortunate that Bryan has been characterized chiefly in connection with the Scopes trial. The Bryan of the trial was not the vigorous, dynamic man of an earlier era. Much of his physical and mental energies had been spent, and Clarence Darrow, the fabled atheistic defense attorney, exploited Bryan unmercifully. According to Linder, the majority of the reporters who covered the trial portrayed Bryan as ignorant and bigoted.

"It is not clear why the contemporary press was so hostile to Bryan and fundamentalism," said Linder. "More study needs to be done to clarify this. Whatever the case, Bryan was misquoted, jeered and vilified in many of the nation's leading newspapers and magazines." The best known of Bryan's detractors was H. L. Mencken of the *Baltimore Evening Sun.* Negative impressions of Bryan were reinforced by a Broadway play in 1959, *Inherit the Wind,* which was made into a movie ten years later.

Perhaps out of intimidation, and perhaps partly out of not understanding how to cope with such allegations in the modern media, the attacks on Bryan went largely unchallenged. As Linder has suggested, some balance on Bryan is long overdue. He says, "As a Christian statesman, he consistently defended personal rather than property rights and championed democracy as the best of all possible forms of government. As a Christian statesman, he opposed war and worked tirelessly for peaceful solutions to world problems. As Secretary of State (1913–1915), Bryan negotiated arbitration treaties with thirty nations. He resigned this position in June, 1915 when he could no longer support President Woodrow Wilson's increasingly belligerent policy toward Germany.

"Further, Bryan was a progressive reformer and a humanitarian because he was an evangelical Christian. To the end of his life, his sense of Christian ethics remained supreme. He believed that the message of Christ was both individual and corporate. He stood for the cross of Christ and against imperialism, alcohol, greed, and godlessness. He believed in both political and economic democracy. He was in the vanguard of the drive for women's suffrage because he believed it was where a Christian belonged. He worked vigorously for change and progress in the political and economic realms, but at the same time he wanted America to remain unchanged morally and theologically."

It is one of the ironies of history that in the name of sophistication Bryan was put down more by the efforts of Mencken than by anyone else while a man, in some respects amazingly similar but of superior intellect, was teaching fundamentalism at Princeton and making church history in the process. Mencken and J. Gresham Machen not only had similar last names. They were both born in Baltimore and were virtually the same age.

The fundamentalist-modernist controversy in which Bryan, Mencken, and Machen were involved undoubtedly was the most influential historical factor in keeping someone who believed like Carter from gaining comparable political stature for a half-century. The dispute centered primarily in churches and seminaries between theological liberals and conservatives, but because it gained widespread attention, many outside these institutions also got into the act.

Toward the end of the nineteenth century, resistance began to develop in the churches and seminaries toward trends in theology which cast considerable doubt on traditional orthodox doctrines. The trends were generally the product of so-called higher criticism which was concerned, not only with the accuracy of text (making sure the content of the Bible today is the same as that of the original, called lower or textual criticism), but also with such things as authorship, form, purpose, and date (called historical or literary criticism). This kind of inquiry was supposedly based on scientific methods whose reliability was more credible than the Bible itself as we know it. Conservatives disputed many of these findings and argued for adherence to core doctrines such as the authority of the Bible and the deity of Christ. By 1918 these basic tenets were being called the fundamentals. In 1920, Curtis Lee

Laws, editor of the Baptist paper *Watchman-Examiner,* started using the terms *fundamentalist* and *fundamentalism.* Laws was part of a "Fundamentalist Fellowship" that believed the liberals, or "modernists," were surrendering the essence of the gospel. This group did not crusade against evolution as is sometimes suggested. Many other conservatives, however, did express considerable concern about the threat that evolutionary teaching represented to biblical truth.

Neither did the Fundamentalist Fellowship identify with the movement known as dispensationalism.* That movement has been popularized in the twentieth century by the *Scofield Reference Bible* and alleged by critics to encourage preoccupation with the hereafter. Its continuing appeal was evidenced by the phenomenal sales of the books by Hal Lindsey such as *The Late Great Planet Earth.*

The Scopes trial in Dayton, Tennessee, climaxed the controversy. Bryan as prosecutor helped to win the conviction of a high-school teacher who taught evolution in violation of a state law. Local sentiment was for Bryan, but on a national and international scale he was vilified.

Part of the stage had been set by an eloquent preacher named Harry Emerson Fosdick who sided with the liberals in the interest of an inclusive church. One of the lesser-known facts in the controversy is that Fosdick had help from a publicity and public relations pioneer named Ivy Lee. The impact of sermons duplicated and distributed by Lee among newspaper editors and other influential people was considerable. Lee was the son of a Georgia Methodist preacher (whose wife was only thirteen when she gave birth to Ivy!).

The whole episode made evangelicals the outsiders even subse-

*So named because it contends that God has divided history into distinct dispensations or economies (usually said to number seven).

quent to the rise of the neo-evangelicals, but gradually the stigma began to wear off. Generations grew up who knew nothing of the controversy and who for different reasons began to question whether science and technology were as much a blessing as their parents had imagined. The Jesus people came onto the scene in the late '60s, and for a time they became the outsiders insofar as evangelicals were concerned.

About this time the evangelical community began to undergo some changes which probably worked to Carter's advantage. Music, forms of worship, and types of prayer were broadened. New kinds of evangelism were adopted. A fresh emphasis on counseling developed. Interpersonal relations took on additional meaning. Doctrinal stands changed very little, but preaching shifted somewhat from the abstract toward the practical. The most profound effects were registered by the charismatic movement which, with its speaking in tongues, rocked the spiritual foundations of thousands of staid old congregations.

Not as noticeable but also significant was the rise of groups of intelligent young Christians who professed to be basically evangelical but who argued for a more radical application of the gospel. Such was the movement started at Trinity Evangelical Divinity School in Illinois under the leadership of Jim Wallis. An articulate if polemical paper published by Wallis was initially named the *Post-American* and renamed *Sojourners* after the group moved to Washington, D.C. Resistance to the group's efforts have come mainly from evangelicals who question whether the conclusions are authoritatively scriptural and exegetically justifiable. Lack of recognition of the American spiritual heritage also alienated establishment-type evangelicals and put the Sojourners in the role of outsiders.

Southern Baptists, who weathered the fundamentalist-modernist controversy remarkably well, have, to a degree, outgrown their outsider role. They participate in the Baptist World Alliance and in the work of the American Bible Society but otherwise are noted for an independent streak that seems to have little to do with either theology or ecclesiology. They simply prefer not to cooperate with other groups either on a local, regional, or national basis. Not even a theological drift to the left in the '60s and '70s made much difference. Southern Baptists have a well-deserved reputation for doing their own thing.

Their indifference to the ecumenical movement is understandable because evangelicals as a whole have stayed at arm's length out of respect to theological differences. But Southern Baptists are outsiders to a degree that they have not wanted to have anything to do with evangelicals in terms of formal fellowship. Some Southern Baptist papers are members of the Evangelical Press Association, and the Southern Baptist radio and television agency has been active in National Religious Broadcasters, but there has been little contact between Southern Baptists and the National Association of Evangelicals.

The denomination is so large, however, that it is difficult to characterize it in an outsider role. Southern Baptists are well enough known and understood that at least among most Protestants Carter's affiliation is more an asset than a liability.

If the ecumenical movement had continued to gain momentum, Southern Baptists might have seen some attraction. Unfortunately, the movement never had any adequate theological grounding and won attention out of sheer sentiment more than anything else. The charismatic movement, although it has proved divisive for many congregations, has also built some bridges. Certainly it has been instrumental in creating a measure of mutual respect between evangelicals and conservative, or charismatic, Catholics.

Carter's sisters are fascinating personalities who might both be classified as outsiders. One of the stories going the rounds during the primaries concerned the sister who travels a great deal. The story appeared in a number of publications. This is how the *National Observer* told it:

She was on her way home to North Carolina, exhausted after three days on the West Coast. She fell gratefully into a seat on the aisle of the DC-8, took off her glasses, put away her books and papers, and snuggled into the cushions to sleep away the tedious hours toward a change of planes at dawn in Atlanta.

The man at the window seat was not sleepy, and he had ideas. He carefully folded his expensively tailored jacket, put it down in the seat between them, and pulled his books and papers *out* of his briefcase. She thought he must be preparing to sell insurance, water-front property in Florida, or aluminum siding. He was, in fact, a salesman. He was selling himself.

He gave her his card and started talking about himself. He had made his first million before he was 30, but his grin and his manner told her that he was prouder still of his skill and grace as a lady-killer. Thirty-two thousand feet over Denver, he suggested a weekend together in the Caribbean. She smiled, and said no.

"But I'll bet you've never gone off for a weekend with a millionaire."

"No, I haven't."

"Are you already involved with a man?" he asked.

"Yes," she said, trying to hide her amusement.

"Are you having an affair with him?"

"No."

"Then who is he? What can he be offering you?"

"His name is Jesus Christ," she said. "Jesus offers me not just a weekend, but a lifetime, and after that, an eternity. He offers it to you, too."

"What are you, some kind of nut?"

"No, not a nut," she said. "I'm what you would call a lady preacher."

"For God's sakes. Oh, sorry, excuse my language, but now you really do have to go away with me. I've never made it with a preacher before."

The woman was Ruth Carter Stapleton, who proceeded straight on home to Fayetteville and her veterinarian husband, Robert, and their family. According to the *National Observer*'s reporter, Wesley Pruden, Jr., the man at the window had vowed before he got off the plane to return to his wife, family, and church. "He teaches a Sunday school class now," Pruden said.

Mrs. Stapleton, five years younger than Jimmy, is one of a kind. Her religious outlook is basically evangelical but more mystical than that of the average Southern Baptist. Moreover, she meshes it with the fruit of thirty graduate credits in psychology and goes around the country lecturing and counseling. She is particularly popular among charismatic groups.

"Ruth works not only with her fellow Protestants but with Roman Catholics," said Ronald Patterson in an article in *Christian Life* magazine. "In fact, she believes that up to this time approximately 60 percent of her ministry has been with the latter."

In 1976 she has campaigned strenuously for her brother and made a speech largely in his behalf at the National Press Club. She is believed to be the first woman preacher to do so in history. The club's luncheon speaker series has been a distinguished forum for the world's most renowned people.

The Carters tend to be close, loyal, and highly supportive of one another's opinions and roles. Ruth and her sister, Gloria, are said to be thoroughly unliberated, however, and disagree with

Jimmy's stand in favor of the Equal Rights Amendment. Gloria's idiosyncrasy, if you consider it that, is that she likes to ride motorcycles. She also talks openly of having had a transforming spiritual experience in 1960. "It sounds so tacky to say reborn or born again, but that's what happened," she said.

Ruth's discussions with Jimmy about his faith, as related by the media, were not strictly along the lines of her "inner healing" specialty. "Basically," wrote Russell Chandler in the *Los Angeles Times,* "her approach is similar to 'primal therapy' (she says she is unfamiliar with it), in which adults are helped to uncover repressed material from their childhood by having them 'regress' and relive the past with as much intensity as they experienced during the original event." She consistently suggests that people recall experiences that hurt them and imagine that this time Jesus is there to help them. Ruth describes her ministry and its positive effects in specific cases in a book she wrote, *The Gift of Inner Healing.*

With Jimmy, it was simply a conversation that the pair had while walking through the woods shortly after he had been defeated in his first bid to become the governor of Georgia. She says Jimmy told her that he had noticed an inner peace about her that he also wanted to have.

Patterson quotes Ruth as saying, "I told him my faith was simple and childlike. I shared my experiences with him and told him that Jesus was not someone who lived 2,000 years ago but was real today, with the power to heal and give peace and serenity. I explained what it meant to be a born-again Christian, and that with this awareness comes strength, stability, and wholeness to life."

Ruth advised Jimmy to rededicate himself to God's work, and shortly after that time Carter began visiting Northern states helping to establish new churches.

Whether commitment to Christ would have an effect upon political possibilities was another matter.

6

To Act Intelligently . . .

ARE EVANGELICALS rational?

"There is a very basic reason why many people distrust an officeholder who has strong religious convictions," a woman wrote in a letter to the editor of the *New York Times*. "There is a concern that the officeholder who is convinced he is doing the right thing because his decisions are God-inspired through prayer may brook no challenge. Who can argue with the self-righteous leader who believes he is listening to and obeying the true word of God?"

That anxiety, expressed in reaction to a story about Carter's religion, could be valid for some religions. Evangelicals, however, believe God has revealed his will in the written Word, the Bible, which is available to all. There are no surprises. Western culture has been built on the precepts of Scripture, and evangelicals campaign for nothing more than biblical ethics. Evangelical Christians disavow anyone who claims on the basis of some pipeline to God that he is being told to violate the Old or New Testaments. The canon has been closed; there is no new revelation.

Some popular misconceptions of evangelical Christianity apparently associate it with irrationality or mysticism because of the question of miracles. Evangelicals differ on whether miracles take place today; this is partly a matter of definition and partly a theological interpretation because some Christians believe the age of miracles to be over. But all evangelicals agree that miracles have taken place, and in the scientifically oriented twentieth century that seems to ask a great deal.

"How very hard it is to be a Christian," says the opening line of Robert Browning's "Easter Day." The deeds are demanding, the dogma even more so. Can modern minds accept miracles? Was Jesus Christ really resurrected? At these junctures many great intellects balk.

The creators of *Godspell* sympathetically and authentically reflect a biblical Jesus, except for the omission of miracles. They take their cue from a host of contemporary theologians who likewise sidestep the resurrection and other similarly astounding phenomena. Their escape route is often to spiritualize the events. If miracle narratives motivate us, why worry about the exact nature of their origins?

One wonders if indeed the effect is the same, let alone honest. The one billion people who now regard themselves as Christians can hardly be rated as living up to their moral potential. The church is in fact plagued with an ethical impotence that may be the result of historical discontinuity. A plant severed from its roots is more likely to attract parasites than to bear fruit. There is no substitute for direct connections with the past.

Close analysis suggests that clouds over the past tend to obscure present ethical responsibilities. Life's most pressing situations invariably prod us to act as realistically as possible. Any sense of right and wrong built on historical uncertainties cannot long endure. Christians in particular need to affix a sticker to the covers of their Bibles: "Void if detached from real life."

A similar problem arises if spiritual concerns are removed entirely from the political realm. A too-strict interpretation of the meaning of church-state separation may limit people to expressing their faith only in abstract, sterile, impersonal contexts which are worlds removed from the things their minds are accustomed to thinking about, and which hardly correspond to the vital ways in which the people of the Bible declared themselves.

Our problems with miracles stem from a contemporary mindset that quite appropriately affirms a high degree of order in the natural universe. But we have carried this kind of thinking to such an extreme that we cannot find a place for nonrepeatable phenomena. We have allowed ourselves to think rationally only about those things common to our experience. In our zeal to eradicate superstition we have in effect placed arbitrary limits upon reality.

In the case of miracles such as the resurrection, documentation of the data is not the primary issue. First, the very possibility must be affirmed. For many scientifically oriented thinkers today, that is too much to handle. In our hearts we may be beginning again to conceive of existences "out there" which we cannot directly comprehend through our senses, but our philosophical framework keeps us from assigning them any standing in the everyday order of things.

Western thought desperately requires a new theory of knowledge that will transcend the immediately apparent. Our sense of values also demands it.

However one views miracles, Carter should not have to be defensive about his priority on intelligent action. He has drawn the attention and admiration of evangelicals who have chafed under an impression that one had to turn off his or her brain to be a Christian. A growing number of evangelicals have been calling for greater consideration to the role of reason in sermons, Bible studies, and literature. The growth of evangelical colleges and seminaries has stimulated demand as graduates return to their churches.

One of the strongest appeals for stressing the place of the mind in the worship and service of God was voiced in an address by John R. W. Stott to the 1972 Inter-Varsity Fellowship annual conference. The address was subsequently published in book form under the title *Your Mind Matters.*

Stott argues for greater Christian recognition of the power of ideas in the world of human action. He quotes Whitehead: "The great conquerors, from Alexander to Caesar, and from Caesar to Napoleon, influenced profoundly the lives of subsequent generations. But the total effect of this influence shrinks to insignificance, if compared to the entire transformation of human habits and human mentality produced by the long line of men of thought from Thales to the present day, men individually powerless, but ultimately the rulers of the world." Stott, an influential evangelical clergyman, contends that churches must encourage great thought if evil in the world is to be confronted adequately.

"Man is able to comprehend the processes of nature. They are not mysterious. They are logically explicable in terms of cause and effect. Christians believe that this common rationality between man's mind and observable phenomena is due to the Creator who has expressed his mind in both. As a result, in the astronomer Kepler's famous words, men can 'think God's thoughts after him.' "

Most great thought in Western culture before modern times came from the minds of Christians. The Puritans, for all their inadequacies, were unusually gifted thinkers. Evangelicals are beginning to counter the notion that a pious Christianity is inevitably linked with shallow emotionalism. "To denigrate the mind," says Stott, "is to undermine foundational Christian doctrines. . . . It is not surprising, in view of these doctrines, to discover how much emphasis Scripture—in both Old and New Testaments—places upon the acquisition of knowledge and wisdom."

The place of the mind in a person's spiritual rebirth is particularly important. J. Gresham Machen expressed it well in *The Christian Faith in the Modern World:* "There must be the mysterious work of the Spirit of God in the new birth. Without that, all our arguments are quite useless. But because argument is insufficient, it does not follow that it is unnecessary. What the Holy Spirit does in the new birth is not to make a man a Christian regardless of the evidence, but on the contrary to clear away the mists from his eyes and enable him to attend to the evidence."

Plato taught that ideal rulers are those who think straight: "Until philosophers are kings, or the kings and princes of this world have the spirit and power of philosophy, and political greatness and wisdom meet in one, and those commoner natures who pursue either to the exclusion of the other are compelled to stand aside, cities will never have rest from their evils,—no, nor the human race, as I believe,—and then only will this our State have a possibility of life and behold the light of day."

Carter is no philosopher, but he does have a sensitivity to the broader issues that few politicians have shown. What overall effect is the nation trying to achieve? How can government best exercise justice? Conscientious attention to such questions can keep the country from drifting into a pragmatic crisis-by-crisis leadership pattern that ends up having little or no principial undergirding.

Carter announced in December 1974 that he was a candidate for the Democratic presidential nomination. He spelled out his rationale at a National Press Club luncheon. At the head table sat Dr. Richard Halverson, pastor of Fourth Presbyterian Church and the foremost evangelical clergyman in the Washington, D.C., area. Carter quoted the Apostle Paul's question, "If the trumpet give an uncertain sound, who shall prepare himself to the battle?" (1 Cor. 14:8). He recited what he felt were some deficiencies of the federal government, then observed, "It is time for us to reaffirm and to strengthen our ethical and spiritual and political beliefs."

Carter called for bridging the "chasm between people and government" and for "an all-inclusive sunshine law in Washington so that special interests will not retain their exclusive access behind closed doors." He proposed what he called "a drastic and thorough revision" of the federal bureaucracy, saying:

"Our nation now has no understandable national purpose, no clearly defined goals, and no organizational mechanism to develop or achieve such purposes or goals. We move from one crisis to the next as if they were fads, even though the previous one hasn't been solved."

Citing the "uncertain sound," Carter went on, "As a planner and a businessman, and a chief executive, I know from experience that uncertainty is also a devastating affliction in private life and in government. Coordination of different programs is impossible." He also urged welfare and tax reform to reduce inequities, more efficiency and less waste in the Pentagon, and arms control with careful implementation.

Carter's Atlanta headquarters put out position papers on most issues, but complaints that his stands were fuzzy persisted through the primary campaign. The matter came to public attention most dramatically when a newly recruited speech writer suddenly quit the staff. Robert Shrum had served only eight days before submitting a letter of resignation telling Carter that he, Shrum, was "not sure what you truly believe in other than yourself."

On closer scrutiny, this kind of charge has often meant not that Carter is failing to take a stand but that he is taking a position between two extremes. On abortion, for example, Carter is quite clear. He says he feels people should not practice abortion and that the government should not encourage it, but that the Supreme Court decision should not be overruled. This has made a lot of pro-life people angry, but his position is clear.

Carter has also taken a somewhat mediating position on détente, urging continued relations with the Communist world but trying to keep negotiations in the open, not yielding more than we receive. Carter also urges cutting back overseas military bases, decriminalizing but not legalizing marijuana, instituting national health insurance, and giving revenue sharing to local governments but not to states. He opposes court-ordered school busing but favors voluntary busing.

He strongly supports the Equal Rights Amendment. He proposes a blanket pardon for draft and military violators from the Vietnam War, his own forgiving spirit having been manifested in employing press secretary Jody Powell, who was evicted from the Air Force Academy for cheating. He supports legislation that would require the registration of handguns and that would ban Saturday-night specials; he also advocates that people convicted of a crime involving a firearm or those "mentally incompetent" be prohibited from possessing a gun.

Carter argues that widespread unemployment is a major reason for continued high inflation and urges that full employment and full production should be the nation's major economic aim. He favors looking first to the private sector of the economy for new jobs. As a last resort,he thinks the federal government should create publicly financed jobs for highway maintenance and construction, mass transit, hospitals, and schools. He has also said "we should consider extension of unemployment compensation, the stimulation of investments, public subsidizing of employment, and surtaxes on excess profits."

In revamping the welfare system, Carter said he would insist that people who *can* work *should* work. People in genuine need should be given continued assistance, he added, but the processes need to be simplified.

Carter has called for developing oil reserves and maintaining imports at manageable levels by government authority when necessary. He also asks that alternative energy resources such as coal and solar energy be developed. He warns against compromising the federal government's commitment to play a significant role in the preservation of natural areas and resources.

What is different about Carter and the issues as distinguished from the run-of-the-mill politician? He feels that people at the grass roots have their own issues agenda that is often ignored. He therefore stresses, for example, his determination to restore honesty to government. Most politicians have not regarded that subject as a concrete issue, but the *Washington Post* published a story March 11 on a poll taken in Florida, two days after the primary there, saying that honesty in government was the single most important issue bothering the voters.

At one point in the primaries, media stories began to suggest that Carter strategy was changing toward greater specificity on public issues. The shift, however, did not represent any major adjustment. Carter had decided long before to stick with a plan that he thought was right and that the people preferred. His approach did not appear to be different from that of John Kennedy in 1960 and Edmund Muskie in 1972. Kennedy's critics charged that he depended on personal appeal and vague promises to rally voters behind him. Some felt that the "Trust Muskie" slogan showed that the senator was waffling.

Alan Ehrenhalf of *Congressional Quarterly* pointed to the success of such approaches at the congressional and state level. He said that perhaps the most significant was Joe Biden of Delaware, who emerged from obscurity in 1972 to win a Senate seat from incumbent Republican J. Caleb Boggs.

"I don't think issues mean a great deal about whether you win or lose," Biden said soon after he was elected. "I think issues give you a chance to articulate your intellectual capacity. Issues are a vehicle by which voters determine your honesty and candor."

The young Biden spent several days with Carter in Atlanta in 1973, and Biden says they found a lot in common. "Carter realized," the senator said, "that it wasn't as important whether you were for or against busing, or abortion, or any issue as whether or not you demonstrated that you were bright and were someone people could trust." Biden eventually became chairman of Carter's national steering committee.

As the primary campaign progressed, Carter said he found it easier to recruit advisers to help him arrive at positions on debatable matters. In the early stages, he said, "it was hard to get people to take me seriously," which meant that stands had to be delayed until some expertise became available.

A report in the *New York Times* said Carter held firm views on a variety of subjects, adding that "it is the manner in which he states them—or keeps silent on them—that the perception of him as opinionless is registered."

The conclusion reached by some voters that Carter talks out of both sides of his mouth was accentuated by another controversial aspect—his repeated promises to be truthful. To his credit he acknowledged several times shading answers to please his audiences. He vowed to desist.

A *Washington Post* editorial defended Carter saying he "tends to give complicated answers to complicated questions—hardly an unforgiveable practice." The *Post* added that conditions in different states "did encourage him to present himself in different ways to different people and interests. We do not think that this is necessarily a damaging or evil or disqualifying thing." The editorial concluded that if he were really being two-faced that fact could be expected to catch up with him.

Columnist Garry Wills also backed up Carter at that point. "One of our ploys," Wills said, "is to hector candidates in the primaries for not taking definitive enough positions; and to say later that they wooed activists in the primaries by taking too strong a stand to survive in the general election."

Carter himself asked to be spared the obligation of spelling out in great detail how he was going to do what he had in mind. Questioned on CBS's "Face the Nation" about specifics on his proposal to cut nineteen hundred federal agencies to two hundred, Carter replied, "There's no way I can take off from campaigning to do a complete and definitive study on what the federal government is and what it's going to be three or four years in the future."

If Carter does have any ambivalence, it probably came out of the differences between his mother and father. His mother has always been decidedly more liberal than her husband was although Carter says that "within our family we never thought about trying to define such labels."

While critics insisted that he had an aversion to stating his position, Carter continued to tell his audiences that "I have never evaded an issue." So the battle raged. Carter urged faith, confidence, self-fulfillment, and trustworthiness while veteran campaigners demanded to know how much federal money he would be willing to risk with financially precarious New York City.

When asked point-blank whether he is a conservative or liberal, Carter replies that on social justice, human rights, and the environment he is "quite liberal." On questions dealing with the management of government, he is "quite conservative."

No small part of Carter's success is attributable to his insight into changes on the American political scene that other, more experienced heads did not immediately sense. One such change is in the various premises associated with liberals and conservatives. The old stereotypes are breaking down, and the citizenry is attaching less significance to the labels.

Before becoming governor, Carter like many Americans looked upon the presidency with a reverence and awe bordering perilously close to idolatry. Television and investigative reporting have helped reduce that tendency, but a surprisingly large number of citizens never see a president close up and certainly have little way of knowing what kind of person he is when he lets his hair down. Carter had seen Harry Truman at a distance. He had never met a president, however, until he was introduced to Richard Nixon. Carter says that during 1971 and 1972 he met Spiro Agnew, George McGovern, Henry Jackson, Hubert Humphrey, Ed Muskie, George Wallace, Ronald Reagan, Nelson Rockefeller, and other presidential hopefuls.

"I lost my feeling of awe about presidents," he states. "This is not meant as a criticism of them, but it is merely a simple statement of fact." To put it a bit more indelicately, he discovered that they were no smarter than he. (Carter has told audiences that he does not claim superior mental capacity to theirs; in joking that many who hear him could possibly qualify as well, he adds that he is glad they did not pick this year to run.)

After nominating Henry Jackson at the 1972 Democratic National Convention, Carter began thinking of himself as a possibility. With his staff, he tried to compare strengths and weaknesses, noting afterward that "the frank assessment of my shortcomings became one of the most enjoyable experiences for my staff, my friends, and my family." The statement, quoted from Carter's autobiography, *Why Not the Best?*, is one of the few attempts at humor in the book.

It is clear that Carter has an amazing number of things going for him in addition to his identification with evangelicals. Carter also foresaw that sectional or geographical prejudice was fading as a political factor. As early as 1960, Kennedy got a bigger margin of victory in his successful campaign for president in Georgia than he did in Massachusetts! Indeed, as racial problems multiplied in the North, there was less finger shaking at the South and perhaps even some extra sympathy for the South to compensate for previous bad feeling. In March 1976, David Broder, the astute political analyst of the *Washington Post,* wrote, "It has been my view for about two years that the Democrats' best bet for victory in 1976 was to nominate a Southerner." There is no doubt that Carter reaped where Wallace sowed, that Wallace brought some issues to the fore at a time when they were not popular, and that with the passing of time these issues were assigned some pivotal significance, particularly in the North, that proved a distinct advantage for Carter.

Strangely enough, on the other side of the ideological spectrum, McGovern was also something of a John the Baptist for Carter. The democratizing process in the Democratic party which enabled McGovern to get the 1972 nomination also enabled Carter to overcome the influence of the big machines. McGovern's "moralizing," which some felt was a major cause of his defeat by President Nixon, may have helped people understand Carter's ethical concerns better than they might have otherwise.

Some feel that Carter is too inexperienced in important modern affairs, but a close look reveals an impressive diversity of interest and practice. *Newsweek* called him the first bionic candidate, but a more fitting description might be that he is the first interdisciplinary candidate. Certainly his farm background equipped him to understand problems related to the production and distribution of food and to understand the balance needed between ecological concerns and technological advance. No small pragmatic consideration was that as a farmer he was willing to face insuperable difficulties and still take a chance even though the future in terms of the weather, the economy, and other variables made it a big gamble. That outlook helped him as a dark-horse candidate.

Carter's military background, his nuclear training and experience, and business involvement are pluses. Most politicians, regardless of party, would agree that leadership of the country desperately needs the kind of planning, management, and goal setting that a good businessman does these days. As Peter Drucker has eloquently pointed out, solving problems only restores normality. "The pertinent question," says Drucker, "is not how to do things right but how to find the right things to do, and to concentrate resources and efforts on them."

The 1976 presidential election was the first subsidized by the federal government, and there is no doubt that this was a major asset for Carter over the other candidates. He would have had a much harder time raising enough money because he was unknown to many key traditional funding sources. Carter also had an unusual amount of financial support from people in his home state who finally saw the prospect of electing the first Southern president in more than a hundred years.

Carter left the governor's office in January 1975, unable by law to succeed himself. With brother Billy running the business in Plains, Jimmy was assured of personal income, so he had the time to campaign for the presidency. No other candidate ever campaigned harder and longer and in more places among more people!

Still another advantage to Carter which "just happened" was that Teddy Kennedy chose not to run although Carter had reportedly assumed that Kennedy would run.

Also particularly useful to Carter were the contacts he had made as chairman of the National Democratic Party 1974 Campaign Committee. It was his responsibility, he said, to learn as much as possible about all the states and congressional districts. "During 1973 and 1974 I met frequently with leaders of groups who ordinarily support Democratic candidates. These leaders, from about twenty-five different organizations, represented labor unions, farmers, Spanish-Americans, teachers, environmentalists, women, local officials, retired persons, government workers, blacks, and the House and Senate campaign committees."

Carter got a firm grasp on the disparate nature of American society, on how many separate special interests are constantly calling for attention, and on how much the country as a whole needs the balance of mediating influences. The risks, he would find, are that go-betweens are readily labeled vacillators. Sometimes, they are even called hypocrites, and in this day and age people seem anxious about hypocrisy to the point of paranoia. Contemporary literature abounds with discussions of hypocrisy. One writer has noted that "the abhorrence of hypocrisy has become almost the ultimate single standard about which twentieth-century man can rally."

A thorough study of the meaning of hypocrisy is long overdue. The term *hypocrisy* seems to suggest something simple, namely, a discrepancy between thought and action. However, even though a pretense of piety or something else understandably arouses revulsion, there is a perspective from which, technically speaking at least, we are all naturally and helplessly "hypocrites." Psychologists teach that every human being plays a number of roles in his or her life and that behavior differs from one role to another. That is obvious when you stop to think about it because we act differently in public, for example, than we do in private. We approach intimate friends in great contrast to the way we deal with bitter enemies. Which is the real us?

Carter has wanted to reach out equally to people who disagree with one another and with him. He does tend to resort to hyperbole, as do most politicians. We need to remember, however, that understatement is no more truth than is overstatement. Missing a target is missing a target no matter the side from which you veer. Exaggeration is easy for speakers whether they be salesmen, preachers, or lawyers; on that score Carter does not deserve to be singled out.

The encouraging thing about Carter in this respect, as reflective of the evangelical ethos and its tenet of original sin, is that he recognizes his bent. His most widely distributed campaign folder quoted him as saying, "There are a lot of things I would not do to be President. If I ever tell a lie, make a misleading statement, avoid a controversial issue, or betray your trust, don't support me." He was asking for scrutiny in his effort to be truthful. As human beings will, he gets defensive when challenged, but his stated long-range intention is soundly ethical and worthy of emulation by other politicians.

Obviously in making more than two thousand speeches during the primary campaign, Carter did not say the same thing in the same way a la tape recorder. Yet in addressing people he must talk at some length about the same topics because that is the only way he can get his message across. The news media can only use snippets of a candidate's remarks and even then only when he says something different. Rarely will a periodical or radio or television station carry the full text of a candidate's remarks; there is just not that much demand for them from the reading public. The candidate on the other hand, must talk about the same things many different times. He cannot always word his remarks exactly the same way, but that does not make him inconsistent. Some biblical critics take a similar tack in saying that there are "differences" among the Gospels of Matthew, Mark, and Luke—and certainly John—because they all describe the life of Jesus but use different phrases and employ different emphases.

The fact is that in American politics anyone at all innovative will have the worst possible construction placed on the results. That's part of the democratic process, however, and we should not knock it.

It is generally assumed both by churchmen and by others that the Bible condemns hypocrisy. Certainly "bearing false witness" or deliberate literal falsehood is evil, but it is not at all clear that what modern users of the English language mean by *hypocrisy* or even *insincerity* falls under that category. The concept of hypocrisy comes from Greek drama and is alien both to Hebrew and to Aramaic, the language Jesus used. English translations of the Bible which use the word *hypocrite* in the Old Testament or in quoting Jesus are at best stretching a point. Originally in the Greek the words *hypocrisy* and *hypocrite* referred to the act of playing a part and the one who plays a part. According to the *Interpreter's Dictionary of the Bible* the terms were also used metaphorically to signify the action of feigning to be what one is not. In English, only the metaphorical meaning remained, with the prevailing signification of the simulation of goodness. "It is unlikely that Jesus in the many passages where he is reported to have attacked the Pharisees as 'hypocrites' was attacking them for simulating goodness . . . Jesus does not attack the Pharisees for insincerity in feigning goodness, though they knew they were evil. On the contrary, it is because they are so self-righteously convinced of their goodness that he castigates them." This authority states that the only passage in the New Testament which clearly retains the original Greek meaning is the verb form used in Luke 20:20, where the scribes and high priests send spies who "pretended to be sincere."

This does not imply biblical license to be two-faced, but it may allow the possibility of wholesome behavior that varies according to time and place.

The Apostle Paul actually told the church at Corinth that he tried to become all things to all people to the extent that he could share with them Christ's saving grace. This does not mean that a person should act in an unprincipled way or compromise Christian principles, but one will sacrifice legitimate personal interests and preferences completely if thereby he or she can provide spiritual assistance.

Who is to say but God when one is a hypocrite? Our overuse of the term probably stems from our overuse of its opposite, namely, sincerity. Probably the most popular theological heresy in the world today is the notion that one believes aright if one is sincere—whatever that means. Sincerity implies correspondence to some basic reality, but the advocates of this heresy (and many are well meaning) don't advertise or define this basic reality. Evangelicals contend that beliefs and behavior must correspond to the written Word of God.

The most serious threat to Carter's campaign came in the form of an article in the March 1976 issue of *Harper's* magazine, "Jimmy Carter's Pathetic Lies." The article, written by Steven Brill, attacked Carter's ethical standards, or rather his alleged lack thereof, charging him with running a dirty-tricks, near-racist campaign to win the governorship in 1970. Although the content had been made public in early February, its effect was not substantial in the New Hampshire primary, but it may well have contributed to Carter's fourth-place finish in Massachusetts the following week. Stormy weather was also a factor in Massachusetts, and Carter commented, "We lost because of the snow, not because of any mud." There were grave fears that the worst fallout would be in Florida because the *Miami Herald,* which is distributed all over the state, ran a condensation.

Harper's charged that Jody Powell, press secretary to Carter, had broken a promise by releasing the content prematurely. Powell issued a detailed twenty-two page rebuttal, and on television

Carter called the article "the most remarkable piece of fiction I've ever read."

An analysis of the whole flap in the July-August issue of *Columbia Journalism Review* by Phil Stanford found that both sides shared blame and that a lot of questions remained unanswered. None of the substantial questions, Stanford said, was original with Brill, and most of them dated from the 1970 campaign.

Stanford also pointed out that the Brill article was curiously ambivalent. Tucked into all the denunciations are such statements as "Carter was a good governor" and "Jimmy Carter has many qualities that could make him a good president."

In the vehement crossfire that followed publication of the article, *Harper's* editor Lewis Lapham said, "Far from being the humble man of the people who promised never to tell a lie, the candidate appeared to be not much different from any other ambitious politician—a man who grinned into the crowds and said whatever enough people wanted him to say."

Numerous comments of a similar nature surfaced throughout the country and demonstrated the most distress over Carter's promise not to lie. The staggering implication in many cases was that it is permissible to lie because everyone else does, as long as you do not lie in saying that you do not lie when you do. A reasonable person scrutinizing this principle is hard-put to figure out its logical basis.

It is certainly fair, proper, and desirable to expect Carter to live up to the high standards he says he has set for himself. He says repeatedly that his aim is to set a good example. Evangelicals who support Carter can help him best by demanding in no uncertain terms that he measure up to what he professes. Carter's aides who have not taken any vow of truth are another story, and evangelicals would do well to suggest strongly that he surround himself with enough people who believe as he does to provide adequate support to do what is right from the strictest possible scriptural standards.

Insofar as the country as a whole is concerned, the task that faces Carter is to deal with the attitude among some that here is just another politician, only this one is using religion to appeal to the people.

7

And Bring America Back Where She Belongs

BLACK PREACHING is a great American art form, far less recognized than it deserves. It combines liturgy and pedagogy with an effectiveness that has few parallels in either sacred or secular tradition.

When the aging Martin Luther King, Sr., rose to give the benediction at the closing session of the 1976 Democratic National Convention, there was not much reason to think his words would be anything but anticlimactic. What little suspense there had been in the convention was resolved with the selection of Senator Walter Mondale of Minnesota as the vice-presidential nominee. The delegates, thankful and happy for a spirit of harmony virtually unprecedented in Democratic history, were now tired almost to the point of giddiness. They were milling about the floor of Madison Square Garden as they had been doing for four days. Only remotely were they aware that one last item remained on the agenda and that it might prove to be at least nostalgic.

True, the delegates for the most part were aware that "Daddy" King was mourning the recent death of a teen-age granddaughter. They all knew he was the father of the civil rights leader slain by an assassin's bullet. Virtually all must have remembered that a younger son had since drowned and that "Daddy" King's wife was subsequently murdered. He was a figure of tragedy, but presidential candidates are a hard act to follow if one is seeking to arrest attention.

King's booming voice called for silence, and in an instant thousands in the hall and millions watching on television were transfixed. He talked briefly. Without being specific, he roared his anguish but also magnified the God who was greater than grief. He called for love, saying "if you have an unforgiving heart, get down on your knees." All this came in thunderous tones that etched their way into the memories of his hearers. Few moments in political history could compare with the high drama of that benediction.

Perhaps his most compelling line was, "Surely the Lord sent Jimmy Carter to come on out and bring America back where she belongs." It was more than an observation. It was a standard going up, a flag to follow, a goal demanding attainment, and a dream to be fulfilled. The style may have gotten in the way for a few who had not been exposed to it before, but for Carter, who grew up close to it, the impact should not have been lost.

Out of the televised (on all three major networks) benediction more people got a taste of black preaching at its best than perhaps ever before. Most whites have known only a comedian's caricature of it. King had come across with the real thing in all its beauty and power.

A number of books have been written about the black preaching tradition, and several authentic stage productions have been attempted. Examples of the sermons themselves are best known through the writings of James Weldon Johnson. Said James S. Tinney in *Christianity Today*, "It forms a special genre of oral literature that goes beyond the usual categories of white homiletics, and that opens up to an even larger realm of subtle chemistries of art and style found only in black churches."

Part of the drama of the occasion, of course, was that King's appearance reminded the delegates present and Americans everywhere of some unfinished business in the realm of justice toward blacks. Sensitivity to racial discrimination in 1976 is not as great as it was several years ago. The selection of King for the convention finale symbolized the fact that after all the effort at party harmony it was necessary to remind the delegates that there is no point in having unity for unity's sake. Human institutions presuppose an active and worthwhile purpose.

The sometimes unfortunate part of that reality, namely that unity needs purpose, is that agreement on purpose invites division. The ecumenical movement found that getting together simply for the purpose of getting together had little lasting appeal. The evangelical community has learned that even trying to cooperate on evangelism represents a monumental task. Focusing on distinctives has the perpetual tendency to put people at odds with one another. Conciliar churches, unable to see eye-to-eye on theological purposes, opted for unity for the sake of coordinated social efforts. These produced a revolutionarylike activism that alienated the grass roots from officialdom in a number of large denominations. The losses are well documented in *Why Conservative Churches Are Growing* by Dean M. Kelley. The people in the pews have been complaining that social action has replaced religious mission, which is what they understood the churches were in existence for in the first place.

Even social activists themselves have begun to realize this. To illustrate the point, Kelley tells of a young lady who had been an organizer for the noted social activist Saul Alinsky for a time. Subsequently she completed law school in order to be able to struggle in the courts for social change. She has little use for churches, says Kelley, "not because they are not radical enough, but because they are not religious enough!" "When my friends want to talk about the meaning of life," he quotes her as saying, "about whether to bring children into the world, we have to gather in one of our homes for a *kaffee klatsch* rather than at the church; the church isn't really struggling with those questions in any way that would help us."

In suggesting the need for clear-cut national goals and objectives, Carter places a large order for himself. What are the United States united *for?* What values underlie that purpose? How much of a consensus is required for genuine, progressive leadership?

Carter did not immediately raise those questions because he knew that prior considerations needed some time to sink in. People needed to be convinced of the need for specific objectives. That is divisive in itself because many humans are quite satisfied to muddle along not quite sure where they are going. Knowledge of destinations is threatening!

What happens more often than not in social human institutions is that the leaders know where they are going but they do not tell their followers. Again, some followers like it that way. Moreover, the leaders do not have to deal with the divisiveness that a revelation of destination brings.

The free enterprise system offers material profit as a goal, and for a substantial part of the population, that is enough. The government does not make the profit itself, but it has traditionally protected that right in America. In recent years all kinds of pressures have been brought to bear on the business community, and more than a few from within it, to reduce the competitive aspects. With the profit motive's loss of standing has come the government's changing role from protector to guarantor.

This shift is regarded by many conservatives as giving the government more power over the lives of the people. Indeed, in the evangelical community the chief anxiety over Carter is that his liberal ideology will result in the loss of liberty. This is a genuine fear that needs to be recognized and taken into account, even if it is thought absurd. But absurd it is not, for any objective survey in America will show increasing regulation of the citizenry. The question is not whether the increase is real but whether it is truly necessary. Thinkers such as B. F. Skinner have argued eloquently that the need for regulation exists, but the answer probably lies with what the people ultimately decide they want the government to be and, possibly even beyond that, whether as the last straw they prefer liberty or death. Not everyone would opt for Patrick Henry's choice.

Like so many life stories of prominent Americans, Carter's recalls the famous nineteenth-century series of books for boys written by Horatio Alger. A Harvard Divinity School graduate, Alger gave up the pastorate of a Unitarian church to become an author. His association in New York City with poor youngsters gave him the background to write the books which focused upon heroes who had come out of humble beginnings. The Alger theme became a symbol and myth because it dramatized the tremendous possibilities for Americans with ability and determination.

On its two-hundredth birthday America faces the question of preserving opportunity or curtailing it. Presidential aspirants are obliged to think about the course they will follow if the electorate assigns them the responsibility of deciding.

In essence, Carter's Baptist background would not have much bearing on things as such. It is interesting to note, however, that only two of the first thirty-seven men to reach the White House were Baptists, despite the preponderance of Baptists in the Protestant community (which has produced all American presidents except one). The first Baptist president was Warren G. Harding, a Republican elected in 1920. The other was Harry S. Truman, a Democrat, who moved into the oval office in 1945.

Carter's hope for a consensus on values lies with a reliance on key aspects of the old Puritan ethic although out of concern that a skeptical public might misunderstand he may be reluctant to admit that hope. Carter does not talk much about bridge building, either, in spite of the fact that as a politician in the South he has been obliged to serve continuously as a mediator. The go-between philosophy is often misunderstood in a country just emerging from a period of extreme polarizations when clear communication was usually taken to consist of exclusivistic definitions. Nixon had talked about bringing the country together again, but immediately upon taking office his vice-president began driving wedges into American society. The *media* that needed to be employed in the *media*ting process were pounced upon, and even though some allegations were valid and needed, at that particular time the effect of their expression was divisive rather than corrective.

In mediating on the basis of classic values which the populace is presumed to have retained, or can be encouraged to recover, Carter will be fulfilling "Daddy" King's prayer to "bring America back where she belongs."

What is a valid base for a national purpose or an ethical system? The evangelical rush for Carter is a corporate suggestion for an answer in spiritual terms. The nation has been experiencing religion on the rebound. Two hundred years after our forefathers established a new nation, evangelicals are ready to assert themselves as perhaps never before, not for odd sectarian practices but for basic Judeo-Christian principles that had previously endured for centuries until pushed aside by the euphoria over science, technology, and materialism. This has not been a mere revival of piety. The prayer breakfasts served their purpose and will continue to do so as stepping stones toward more profound expressions of faith. A more mature understanding of biblical precepts would implement a concern for all aspects of life on earth.

A man from Plains speaks of his new birth, and the country is seeking one. The evangelical ethos, hidden and scorned for years, is surfacing with a freshness that appeals to the times.

Martin Marty was asked whether Jimmy Carter's talk about the evangelical experience could be authentic because "no one in our office has ever met anyone who ever talks that way." Evangelicals have been there all the time but quite uncertain whether it was desirable that they be heard from. Before women's liberation and even afterward, it had been a mark of "masculinity" not to talk of religion. It was the ultimate put-down, even in learned journals, to note that Soviet Christians were a weak group because their congregations were composed predominantly of older women.

Evangelicals out in the sunshine again is not by any means altogether their own doing. A growing element of secular sophistication tolerates and respects evangelicals. One analyst wonders if things are not going too far. "Although evangelical Protestantism has a great deal more to it than Menckenesque contempt allows," he said, "still it shouldn't be romanticized by remote cosmopolitans."

In a real sense, it is a welcome sight to behold a Puritan-oriented evangelical ethos that emphasizes highly disciplined living, trained minds, hard work, good management, and conscientious attention to personal piety and social behavior. Such a suggestion likely strikes terror into the minds and hearts of people conditioned to think of Puritans wholly in terms of repression and as a group lacking in a sense of humor or enjoyment of life. Puritans have been worked over long enough, however, and it is time to see the positive side of their philosophy and accomplishments and to begin to appreciate the fact that they had a handle on happiness that the twentieth century has not even begun to explore.

Civil religion has been a controversial topic of the late '60s and '70s primarily because of its association with evangelicals. Evangelicals and others have denounced the concept, or rather a concept by that name, inasmuch as there are varying definitions of what people are talking about when they say civil religion. The fear is that evangelical patriotism slides into a worship of Americanism. It may be that evangelicals have put too high a priority on national interests, but there has been little evidence that the respect of country has been on a worship level and that this respect has been a religion in any technically acceptable sense. To be so it would have to be "country over God."

Talk of civil religion nearly always brings up an association with a religious national consensus and the fact that that is bad. But some scholars led by Richard Neuhaus are calling for something like civil religion as a way of renewing America's spiritual heritage. Neuhaus, who would not call himself a conservative evangelical, nonetheless senses the strengths of this ethos when he calls for consideration of "the unexamined resources in a tempered Puritanism."

Reconsidering that a nation like an individual may have a religion and not know it leaves only the question of what that religion will be. Avoiding a nuclear war can be a civil religion if enough people assign enough priority to the concern.

Addressing a religious bicentennial conference, Neuhaus urged Americans to "disabuse ourselves of the fear of religious zealots eager to take over the state in order to enforce their beliefs on the populace."As a matter of history, he suggested, "It was probably the experience of mutual toleration among religionists, more than the external checks imposed by secularists, that established tolerance in the civil realm." He predicted that the cultural assertiveness of religion will become a growing force in shaping our common future.

The changing attitude of the Jewish community is said to be one example of the trend away from secularism in American life. Thirty years ago, Neuhaus said, "it seemed to many that the security and prosperity of Jewry would be best assured by a thoroughly secularized society, at least in the public realm. Today that does not seem so evident."

Among the reasons for this change of attitude, he commented, is that "in a thoroughly secularized society there is no final, absolute barrier against evil, including the evil of anti-Semitism."

One way of looking at the new religious picture is to describe it as going the way of sex. People for the most part have been as uncomfortable in talking of personal religious experience as they used to be in discussing the more intimate aspects of the procreative process.

Until recently, as Christians and Jews maintained walls of privacy around their innermost beliefs, religion cropped up in conversation only in broad, abstract terms. A personal religious discussion tended to focus on ethical issues on a social scale or on major controversies such as whether priests should marry or women should be ordained.

Ask someone, Are you saved? and the reaction would border on trauma.

We were culturally conditioned to believe that the precise nature and extent of one's faith was so personal that any attempt to transcend it was unwarranted intrusion. One's relationship to God was regarded as such an intangible that he or she could do little more than joke about it. Even churchgoers were often cynical about the individual spiritual state and the prospect of life after death.

Many people obviously still feel this way, but a fresh openness to deal with spiritual realities has been developing steadily.

Evangelicals did not respond to Jimmy Carter because he was initiating a revival of piety. A new spiritual reality was already there—in him and in the nation.

There is, in short, a growing aversion to hiding one's spiritual light under a bushel. Sinners are again walking the sawdust trail, not in camp meeting tents but in the context of various public and private exposures that are every bit as real.

Carter has performed the favor of introducing Americans to one another—Southerners to Northerners, farmers to engineers, young to old, men to women, outsiders to insiders, scholars to activists, Christians to non-Christians, and so on.

Evangelicals, for their part, can return the favor by developing a social systematic that summons the best of the past for a confrontation with tomorrow. Regeneration is the basic equipment because it changes people and shares the potential that built Western culture. The evangelical ethos has served the United States well, but the people of the twentieth century want a more sophisticated rationale.

In the thirteenth century, Thomas Aquinas as a Christian faced a pluralism as we do today. The great minds of the Muslim world were appropriating Aristotle and seemed to be on their way toward dominating the thought of the West. Thomas could appeal to scriptural authority in addressing secular man no better than we can. His defense which carried the day against Islam was "natural theology"—tenets built on observable phenomena regarded as demonstrable in themselves without appeal to revelation. God revealed himself to an extent in these phenomena, but the Scriptures were necessary for full knowledge of what he wanted people to know about him.

The tensions between Protestants and Catholics brought about by the Reformation have worked against adequate appreciation of Thomistic thought, and evangelicals are skeptical of natural theology. Indeed, it may have preceded or even precipitated the modern distinction between public and private faith although evangelicals speak of general and special revelation. What is needed, it seems, is what Francis Schaeffer has been stretching for, a belief system attractively authenticating and commending itself as an ethical philosophy adequate for the problems of the day and fulfilling for the human beings who face them. Evangelicals owe at least that much to their God, their country, and such people in public service as Jimmy Carter.

The lesson used by the men's class that hot Sunday morning was the last in the book. It closed with a paragraph, "You and 1776," asking, "Would love for others cause you to work for good government? What would you have done if you had been in the position of Samuel Adams, Benjamin Franklin, Patrick Henry, or George Washington?"

The last sentence is fitting for Carter, for his Sunday school class, for other Christians, indeed, for all American people: "Perhaps the most important question is what you will do now to make these United States 'one nation under God with liberty and justice for all.' "

Epilogue

"Skies were clear throughout most of the country yesterday—unusual for an election day," the *New York Times* reported on November 3, 1976. Precipitation was limited to five or six states. All states except Alaska reported temperatures well above freezing the day people cast their ballots. Early in the evening Atlanta and Minneapolis were both recording fifty degrees. Weather conditions were remarkably conducive to a large voter turnout and undoubtedly helped to offset the mood of indifference sensed by many during the campaign itself. Some further motivation was provided by the closeness of the preelection polls. The major surveys on election eve had reflected a virtual dead heat.

James Earl Carter, Jr., was elected the thirty-ninth president of the United States with 50.1 percent of the vote. The incumbent, President Ford, got 48 percent.

The popular vote totals showed Carter with 40,828,487, Ford with 39,147,613, and 1,574,971 going to others.

The Carter-Mondale Democratic ticket collected 297 electoral votes. Ford and his vice-presidential running mate, Senator Robert Dole of Kansas, tallied 241 as the Republican nominees.

Former Senator Eugene McCarthy of Minnesota failed to pick up any electoral votes, but as a third-party candidate for president he made enough of a showing in several states to threaten the overall outcome. Primarily because he had previously been a major Democratic figure, McCarthy cut into Carter more than into Ford. Had McCarthy's name been allowed on the ballot in New York, he might well have reduced Carter's total there enough to swing the state's forty-one electoral votes—and therefore the whole election—to Ford. A last-minute court appeal by McCarthy to get his name on the ballot in New York was rejected.

Carter's margin in the polls had dwindled steadily during the campaign, but the Georgian kept his composure throughout. The highly methodical style of the primaries was simply extended into the ultimate showdown.

If the grind ever got to him, Carter never publicly showed it. Only for a brief moment after victory was assured did emotion dominate. That was at dawn on November 3 when Carter and his family flew back to their home in Plains and were greeted by several hundred townspeople in front of the old railroad station that had been converted into a campaign headquarters. Said Carter, "I came all the way through—through 22 months and I didn't get choked up until I . . . "

At that his eyes filled with tears and he embraced his wife Rosalyn who also wept. Carter quickly recovered ana went on, "until I turned the corner and saw you standing here and said, 'People who are that foolish—we can't get beat.' "

The crowd had waited all night for him. Carter watched the returns on television at a hotel in Atlanta. By midnight in the East he seemed to be within one or two states of certain election, but it was several hours before a clincher was apparent.

By many counts, it was the Mississippi result that finally gave Carter the 270 electoral votes needed to win. The outcome in Mississippi, decidedly a Bible-belt state, hinged to a great extent on how voters reacted to the celebrated interview of Carter in *Playboy* magazine. Carter got a big boost when Owen Cooper, noted Mississippi industrialist and churchman, came to his defense. Cooper lamented a vulgarity attributed to Carter, but on the whole found the interview theologically sound. Cooper said the article amounted to a Christian witness in a medium that needed it. He said he would always try to sell his products to businesses that needed them. "I'd go where there's a scarcity. . . . If Christ were given the opportunity of writing an article for *Christianity Today,* which is read by most conservative theologians, or *Playboy,* which would He choose? I leave you to answer that, but I think it was an appropriate article in an appropriate medium."

Cooper's remarks were thoroughly covered by the Mississippi media and undoubtedly had influence also in neighboring states, particularly because Cooper was widely known in church circles, having served two years as president of the Southern Baptist Convention.

Church people who would have otherwise been supportive of Carter were troubled, not only by the *Playboy* interview, but by the Democratic platform on abortion, which was more permissive than the Republican. Carter himself says he is personally against abortion but does not favor a constitutional amendment to override the U. S. Supreme Court decision of 1973 which struck down state antiabortion laws. The record of the Ford administration did not please antiabortion forces either, and one member of the electoral college in the state of Washington who was supposed to vote for Ford cast his ballot instead for Reagan as a protest abortion policy.

The Sunday before the election another crisis arose that might have had an effect on the voting. A black clergyman from Albany, Georgia, appeared in Plains to seek membership in Carter's church. Deacons, uncertain as to the motivations of the would-be member, canceled services and called for the resignation of their pastor because he had favored consideration of the outsider, the Rev. Clennon King. Carter was not in town that weekend but subsequently went to work behind the scenes. The pastor, the Rev. Bruce Edwards, got a vote of confidence from the congregation. A committee was named to "test the sincerity of all persons applying for membership and make recommendations to the church." Most significantly, by a vote of 121 to 66, a motion was adopted to "open the church to all persons, regardless of race."

Index

Abernathy, Ralph 38
Abortion 90–91, 121
Agee, James 26
Alger, Horatio 138
Alinsky, Saul 137
Anderson, Patrick 31–32
Aquinas, Thomas 21, 143
Aristotle 21
Atlanta 18, 27, 30
Atlanta Constitution 83
Atlanta Journal 34

Bagley, Smith 100–102
Bailey, Nathan 67
Baker, Russell 99
Baltimore Evening Sun 107
Barth, Karl 20, 21
Biden, Joe 122–123
Blacks 10, 15, 26, 41, 88, 96, 100, 134–136
Blanchard, Jonathan 43
Bourne, Peter 97
Bowen, Catherine Drinker 9
Briggs, Kenneth 8
Brill, Steven 131–132
Broder, David 126
Brow, Robert 58
Brown, Jerry 6, 98
Brown, William Burlie 8, 47
Browning, Robert 116
Bryan, William Jennings 47, 105–109

Callaway, Howard (Bo) 39–40
Calvin, John 21, 61, 84
Carter, Billy 17, 127
Carter, Hugh 2
Carter, James Earl, Sr. 17, 30
Carter, Lillian Gordy 14, 29–30, 32
Carver, George Washington 29
Catholics 10, 12, 15
Chandler, Russell 114
Charismatic Movement 111
Christian Century 8, 22, 54
Christian Herald 36
Christian Life 14, 42, 113–114
Christianity and Crisis 22
Christianity Today 49, 53, 65, 72–74, 106, 136, 147
Church, Frank 100
Civil Religion 24
Clifford, Clark 100
Cohen, Richard 94

Coleman, Julia 16
Colson, Charles 72–75, 78
Columbia Journalism Review 132
Columbus, Christopher 59, 60
Conscience 13
Constantine 56
Cooper, Owen 147
Cromwell, Oliver 9
Cronkite, Walter 102
Cruz, Eloy 39

Darrow, Clarence 106–107
Davis, A. D. 31
Dayton, Donald W. 43
Dispensationalism 109
Dodson, Clarence 3
Donaldson, Sam 2, 3
Drucker, Peter 127

Economist of London 105
Edwards, Bruce 148
Edwards, Jonathan 9, 65, 66
Ehrenhalf, Alan 122
Eisenhower, Dwight 25, 92
Eisenstat, Stuart 11
Eliot, John 63
Evangelical Ethos 53, 59, 60–67, 70, 96, 129, 140
Evans, Rowland 90

Farming 27–28
Finney, Charles G. 43
Fletcher, Joseph 76–77
Ford, Gerald 5, 24, 98, 145
Fosdick, Harry Emerson 109
Frankfurter, Felix 106
Fritchey, Clayton 100
Fundamentalist-Modernist Controversy 108

Gardner, John 100
Germond, Jack W. 94–95
Gilmore, J. Herbert 80
Gordy, Jim Jack 30
Graham, Billy 5, 36, 42, 96
Graham, Katharine 100
Grogan, G. W. 14
Gunter, William 19

Halverson, Richard 119–120
Handel, G. F. 50
Harding, Warren G. 139
Harper's 131–132
Hartford Declaration 88
Hatfield, Mark 78
Hefley, James C. 62, 77
Henry, Carl F. H. 81
Holifield, E. Brooks 16, 19, 21, 66
Hughes, Harold, 77, 90
Hunt, Robert 62
Hypocrisy 128–131
Huss, John 48

Irwin, Grace 26

Jefferson, Mildred F. 90
Jews 9–12, 142
Johnson, James Weldon 136
Johnson, Lyndon 94
Jones, Howard 36

Kelley, Dean 24, 136
Kennedy, Edward 100, 127
Kennedy, John F. 48, 89, 122
Key 73 52
King, Clennon 148
King, Martin Luther, Sr. 134–136, 139
Kraft, Joseph 70

Lapham, Lewis 132
Laws, Curtis Lee 108–109
Lee, Ivy 109
Lewis, C. S. 72, 74
Linder, Robert D. 105–108
Lindsell, Harold 20
Lindsey, Hal 109
Lippmann, Walter 99
Lipshutz, Robert 11
Locke, John 66
Los Angeles Times 113
Luther, Martin 61, 83

McCarthy, Eugene 146
McGovern, George 67, 126
Machen, J. Gresham 99, 108, 119
Maddox, Lester 40
Magruder, Jeb 76

Marty, Martin 54, 140
Marx, Karl 21
Mayflower Compact 63
Mencken, H. L. 107, 108, 140
Menninger, Karl 87
Miami Herald 131
Miller, Perry 65
Miller, William Lee 25
Mondale, Walter 134, 145
Morgan, Marabel 78
Morison, Samuel Eliot 35, 59, 65
Moyers, Bill 16, 80, 98
Muggeridge, Malcolm 88
Murray, Alice 83–84
Mystical Body 6

National Courier 24, 68–69
National Observer 112
Neo-evangelicalism 20
Neo-orthodoxy 19–20
Neuhaus, Richard 141–142
New Republic 16, 66
Newsweek 47, 90, 126
Newton, Jim 13, 69
Newton, John 26
New York 9, 75
New York Times 8, 97, 115, 123, 145
New York Times Magazine 31–32
Niebuhr, Reinhold 16–22
Nixon, Richard 72, 75, 76, 94, 95
Noll, Mark 65
Noll, Stephen 24

Novak, Michael 95–96
Novak, Robert 90

Ockenga, Harold John 20
Olmstead, Clifton E. 61
Osmond, Donny and Marie 85

Pacifism 16
Patterson, Ronald 113–114
Pell, Claiborne 100
Pennington, John 34
Phillips, Tom 72
Playboy interview 147
Plowman, Edward E. 77
Populism 16
Powell, Jody 121, 131
Prayer 2, 5, 68, 69, 110
Pruden, Wesley, Jr. 113
Puritans 9, 18, 35, 48, 53, 95, 118, 139, 140–141

Rader, Paul 76
Rafshoon, Gerald 76
Rauschenbusch, Walter 36
Reagan, Ronald 5, 98, 125
Reeves, Richard 9, 75
Religious Issue 5–14, 23
Ribicoff, Abe 10
Rickover, Hyman G. 103
Roosevelt, Franklin Delano 17, 28
Rule, Gordon W. 104
Ryskamp, Henry J. 84

Schaeffer, Francis 144
Schlesinger, Arthur, Jr 16
Sevareid, Eric 100
Sherrer Quin 68–69
Shrum, Robert 120
Situation Ethics 76
Skinner, B. F. 138
Skinner, Tom 36
Smith, Elwyn A. 12
Social Gospel 36
Sojourners 114
Solzhenitzyn, Alexander 88
Southern Baptist Convention 147
Stanford, Phil 132
Stapleton, Ruth 17, 46, 111–114
Stott, John R. W. 118
Stroud, Kandy 1

Tanenbaum, Marc H. 10
Theology Today 77
Tillich, Paul 55, 77
Time 8, 23, 47
Timmerman, Cody 2
Tinney, James S. 136
Tolstoy, Leo 16
Truman, Harry 10, 125, 139
Tuchman, Barbara 10

Vocation 79–85

Wall, James M. 22
Wallace, George 6, 22, 125

Wallis, Jim 110
Washington Post 25, 46, 70, 94, 95, 99, 122, 126
Washington Star 1, 94
Watchman-Examiner 109
Whitehead, A. N. 118
Wilberforce, William 43
Williams, Robert 35
Williams, Tennessee 94
Willkie, Wendell 106
Wills, Garry 124
Wilson, Woodrow 107
Wise, P. J. 2
Witcover, Jules 46
Women's Liberation 121, 140

Zinzendorf, Count Nikolaus von